Praise for **PIVOTAL**

"Shapiro has written a grounded book for dizzying times. His simple yet profound framework combines stability and agility to offer a wise alternative to perpetual pivoting that can help you build an iconic, enduring business."

—DANIEL H. PINK, #1 *New York Times* bestselling author of *Drive, The Power of Regret,* and *To Sell Is Human*

"Innovation has become the default—but what happens when innovation becomes the enemy of quality and focus? Steve Shapiro's *Pivotal* focuses on not just what it takes to change the game, but when and if change is even necessary. Rethinking the efficacy of the terminology and practices that maintain the status quo, Shapiro encourages a future that thinks more critically and keeps substance at the forefront."

—DR. MARSHALL GOLDSMITH, Thinkers50 #1 Executive Coach and *New York Times* bestselling author of *The Earned Life, Triggers,* and *What Got You Here Won't Get You There*

"'Read not the Times. Read the Eternities.' Henry David Thoreau wrote that bit of timeless advice in 1863, a good 150 years before social media and today's hustle culture took over. Like Thoreau, Stephen Shapiro understands that in a future obsessed with the next big thing, *Pivotal* readers will differentiate themselves by rejecting the cult of distraction and doubling down on substance and depth."

—MIKE BECHTEL, Chief Futurist, Deloitte Consulting; Adjunct Professor of Corporate Innovation, University of Notre Dame

"Pivoting is all the rage among start-ups. But Shapiro makes clear that pivoting without differentiation and stable capabilities is a fast turn to nowhere. If your business environment is changing—and whose isn't?—you need to read this book."

—THOMAS H. DAVENPORT, Distinguished Professor, Babson College; MIT Research Fellow; author of *Competing on Analytics* and *All-in on AI*

"Technology and AI are changing the game for every organization, and Shapiro's important insight is the power of focusing on what doesn't and shouldn't change. His mantra, 'innovate where you differentiate,' is not just advice; it's a strategic imperative for thriving in today's dynamic, turbulent world. *Pivotal* provides a road map for leaders seeking to drive reinvention while holding fast to what is truly unchangeable."

    —PAUL DAUGHERTY, Chief Technology and Innovation Officer, Accenture

"In today's fiercely competitive entrepreneurial landscape, standing out is not just important—it's essential. Shapiro's *Pivotal* elevates the conversation from mere differentiation to a masterclass on becoming irreplaceable. This book is more than a read; it's a potent catalyst for career transformation."

    —DORIE CLARK, *Wall Street Journal* bestselling author of *The Long Game* and executive education faculty, Columbia Business School

Stephen M. Shapiro

PIVOTAL

CREATING
STABILITY
IN AN
UNCERTAIN
WORLD

amplify
an imprint of Amplify Publishing Group

www.amplifypublishinggroup.com

Pivotal: Creating Stability in an Uncertain World

©2024 Stephen M. Shapiro. All Rights Reserved. No part of this publication may be reproduced, stored in a retrieval system or transmitted in any form by any means electronic, mechanical, or photocopying, recording or otherwise without the permission of the author.

The views and opinions expressed in this book are solely those of the author. These views and opinions do not necessarily represent those of the publisher or staff. The publisher and the author assume no responsibility for errors, inaccuracies, omissions, or any other inconsistencies herein. All such instances are unintentional and the author's own.

For more information, please contact:
Amplify Publishing, an imprint of Amplify Publishing Group
620 Herndon Parkway, Suite 220
Herndon, VA 20170
info@amplifypublishing.com

Library of Congress Control Number: 2024900990

CPSIA Code: PRV0324A

ISBN-13: 979-8-89138-002-8

Printed in the United States

To all the individuals and companies I've worked with over the years. Your stories, struggles, and insights have been my greatest teachers.

CONTENTS

PREFACE	ix
Introduction	xi

Section One:
Know Where to Go Deep

CHAPTER 1
Being Pivotal Is Not About Pivoting 1

Chapter 2
Let's Get Pivotal 15

Section Two:
Innovate Where You Differentiate

Chapter 3
The Three Levels of Capabilities 27

Chapter 4
The Innovation Targeting Matrix 39

Section Three:
The 5Ds of Differentiation

Chapter 5
Today, Tomorrow, and Leverage 51

Today

Chapter 6
Distinctive 61

Chapter 7
Desirable 73

Tomorrow

Chapter 8
Durable — 97

Chapter 9
Dynamic — 107

Leverage

Chapter 10
Disseminated Internally — 123

Chapter 11
Disseminated Externally — 135

Section Four: Beyond the Organization

Chapter 12
It's About the Individual — 149

Chapter 13
Differentiation for Employees — 153

Chapter 14
Differentiation for Entrepreneurs — 157

Chapter 15
Differentiation in Your Personal Life — 161

FAST Innovation® — 167

Why Innovation Is So Important to Me—and the World — 173

Continue the Journey — 179

About the Author — 183

Acknowledgments — 185

PREFACE

Let's face it: the business world is tumultuous. Changes are constant, distractions are everywhere, and every day presents a choice that could elevate your company or derail it.

We live in an era where uncertainty is the norm. New opportunities and challenges bombard us daily, making it more difficult than ever to know which direction to turn. Although predicting the future in this volatile environment is nearly impossible, establishing a solid foundation that fosters stability, depth, and value is achievable.

Rather than pivoting, it's about becoming pivotal.

To be pivotal, you must become irreplaceable and indispensable to your customers and provide clarity and direction to your employees. It means discerning genuine opportunities from mere distractions. Most importantly, it involves knowing where to channel your resources for the greatest impact.

> "There's a question that comes up very commonly: 'What's going to change in the next five to ten years?' But I very rarely get asked, 'What's not going to change in the next five to ten years?'"
>
> —Jeff Bezos

Jeff Bezos, the founder, executive chairman, and former president and CEO of Amazon, summarized this concept beautifully in his 2007 *Harvard Business Review* interview. He said, "There's a question that comes up very commonly: 'What's going to change in the next five to ten years?' But I very rarely get asked, 'What's not going to change in the next five to ten years?' At Amazon we're always trying to figure that out, because you can really spin up flywheels around those things. All the energy you invest in them today will still be paying you dividends ten years from now."

Paying dividends today, tomorrow, and ten years from now is the goal.

And this book is designed to arm you with strategies to do just that. But the learning shouldn't stop here. Share your insights with others on your team, and implement the approaches.

For more actionable tools and frameworks, visit

www.ThePivotalTools.com

There you will find complimentary resources designed to further your understanding and help you become truly pivotal in today's business landscape.

Here's to your pivotal journey. Welcome aboard.

INTRODUCTION

Championing the Planted Foot

Silicon Valley startup Homejoy looked like a clear winner. A promising platform that connected customers with professional cleaners in thirty-five cities across the United States, Canada, the United Kingdom, and Germany, it offered a nineteen-dollar-per-cleaning price point for first-time customers, while others were charging upwards of eighty dollars. This low-cost strategy enabled the company to quickly grow its customer base to 1.5 million, raising a whopping $40 million in funding.

The founders used that funding to make an ambitious shift. They would no longer confine themselves to cleaners but would expand into other home services, such as plumbing and handyman work. This would allow Homejoy to increase revenue opportunities with existing customers. It was, by all appearances, a strategy that couldn't lose.

But it did lose. In fact, it was a disaster.

As it turns out, the low price point that initially attracted so many customers also led to low profit margins and high customer acquisition costs. Homejoy's lack of loyal customers made maintaining sustainable growth and revenue difficult, with less than 20 percent of customers becoming repeat users.

To make matters worse, Homejoy also struggled to retain a stable workforce of cleaners. Many cleaners left after finding better opportunities elsewhere or becoming dissatisfied with the company's policies, including low pay, unreliable scheduling, and lack of support from Homejoy's staff.

Homejoy's shift to offer additional home services only added to its problems. Although this move was an attempt to diversify its revenue streams and compete with other platforms like Handy, TaskRabbit, and Thumbtack, it diluted Homejoy's brand identity—being a reliable and affordable home cleaning service—and quality control.

Moreover, expanding to other services required more resources and expertise than Homejoy had. Homejoy had to recruit, train, manage, and support more workers with different skills and backgrounds, ultimately dealing with more complex logistics and regulations for different types of services. These challenges required more resources and expertise than Homejoy had, and the underlying issues of low worker and customer retention were not addressed.

Ultimately, Homejoy's addition of other services and expansion into additional geographies were distractions from rather than a solution to its core problems. Its low-cost strategy, as implemented, was not sustainable. All of this led to Homejoy's ultimate demise in July 2015, just five years after launch.

The Homejoy story underscores the risks of not having a viable differentiator before making strategic shifts. While they believed that branching into new areas would benefit them, they overlooked the fact that their core business wasn't yet sustainable. Introducing more change merely accelerated their decline, as they lost sight of what truly mattered. I raise the story of Homejoy because their dilemma is one we all face: Should we build upon our successes or explore new horizons?

Compare Homejoy's approach with that of Mercadona, the leading discount retailer in Spain. While both adopted a low-cost strategy, Mercadona viewed it as a strength and chose to double down on it rather than explore new opportunities. When the 2008 recession struck, instead of cutting wages or reducing staff like many others did, Mercadona tapped into the relationship they had cultivated with their employees over the years. The company encouraged workers to identify other nonlabor cost savings. Through this approach, they reduced prices by 10 percent while strengthening the commitment of their employees. This ultimately led to their market share growing from 15 percent in 2008 to 20 percent in 2012. This approach not only enhanced service and productivity but also yielded benefits that persisted long after the crisis subsided.

Their approach was markedly different from competitors who cut wages and reduced employee hours. This typically resulted in poorly maintained stores, subpar customer service, disengaged employees, and a weakening of their brands.

Instead of placing new bets in new areas, Mercadona doubled down on its low-cost differentiation. And rather than alienating employees, they chose to invest in them through education and cross-training. Homejoy could have been successful had they used a similar playbook. They could have improved their relationship with their workforce rather than treating them poorly. They could have doubled down on their existing business model, leveraging their large price-sensitive customer base. Instead, they chose to ignore their existing issues and focus on new investments. This diversification ultimately dissipated its focus.

Homejoy's expansion into new geographies and diverse offerings could be described as a pivot since it marked a change in its business strategy. And while such a change isn't inherently negative, Homejoy lacked a stable footing upon which to base these shifts. This book emphasizes the importance of establishing a solid foundation for your business before diverting your focus to new products, services, or offerings. Double down on what matters most. In a world brimming with opportunities and distractions, distinguishing between the two is essential. Not all changes are necessarily good, and staying the course doesn't mean that you're standing still.

The Power of the Planted Foot

Enter the notion of the planted foot. Picture a basketball player executing a pivot. While one foot moves in a circular motion, the other remains anchored to the ground. The unsung hero is the foot that doesn't move, providing the solid foundation and stability needed for effective pivots. In the context of innovation, this planted foot represents the deep, unyielding roots of history, customer insights, product knowledge, and trust that give us the foundation from which to navigate change.

> In a world brimming with opportunities and distractions, distinguishing between the two is essential. Not all changes are necessarily good, and staying the course doesn't mean that you're standing still.

This book champions the power of the planted foot, teaching you how to cultivate lasting relationships with your market to create enduring value. By focusing on what doesn't (and shouldn't) change, you build a robust foundation that supports future shifts, without wasting valuable resources on fleeting fads or needless upheaval. Plant, *then* pivot.

The emphasis has always been on what's next. But sometimes we need to focus on what's now. Where do we double down our efforts to achieve extraordinary returns today and tomorrow?

> The emphasis has always been on what's next. But sometimes we need to focus on what's now.

Being pivotal comes from a place of power. Being pivotal is about deepening relationships with your market to create long-term, sustainable value. Although it might appear that Homejoy was deepening its relationship with its customers by offering a wider range of services, this diversification was not built on a foundational differentiator. They never addressed the fundamental flaws of their business model. Rather than being a strategic move, it was driven by the all-too-common Silicon Valley mindset of "grow at any cost." They were pivoting before becoming pivotal.

You need different skills to live in the world of the planted foot as an innovator. With the moving foot, you must be able to see ahead. Predict the future. Ride the waves of fads and trends. It is difficult because, without your crystal ball, you might be making wrong decisions at every turn.

But the planted foot cares about stability and provides the vantage point from which to see ahead. It cares about depth and relationships. You're in it for the long haul. Instead of shallow and shifting, this foot is deep and rooted.

It's important to note that the planted foot is not inherently better than the one moving in circles. It's not about stability versus movement. You need both. Long-term success and enduring competitive advantage are achieved by striking the right balance between movement and steadfastness.

> Being pivotal comes from a place of power. It is about deepening relationships with your market to create long-term, sustainable value.

This book provides guidance on how to identify the areas where you and your organization should focus your efforts to deepen your roots. The concepts within provide a foundation that allows you to get leverage while also positioning the other foot for a shift when needed.

Pause the Perpetual Pivoting

Newton's first law of motion states that a body in motion stays in motion. The business corollary is that a business in motion stays in motion.

Although the concept of pivoting has been a part of business for decades, its pace was significantly accelerated by the pandemic that began in 2020. This rapid shift introduced a whirlwind of change, leaving uncertainty in its wake. The dizzying movement from such relentless pivoting has become an endemic aspect of business. As predicted by Newton's law, momentum propels this change forward, and it shows no signs of stopping.

Of course, there are times when pivoting is necessary. But an environment of constant change can be exhausting and unproductive. Moreover, pivoting on quicksand provides no stability for the organization. You can't move forward when you're stuck swirling.

It is for this reason that I wrote *Pivotal*. I saw the uncertainty and worry in the eyes of my clients as they wondered which changes to make next: Where should we invest to make the most significant impact? How much should we focus on emerging technologies such as artificial intelligence (AI) or the metaverse? What changes should we make to remain relevant in an unpredictable environment? Regrettably, many opportunities were just distractions in disguise.

I also saw the negative impact of this nonstop spinning on the employees. Change fatigue and a lack of consistent direction created burnout, confusion, and disengagement.

This book is the antidote to incessant pivoting. To be clear, I'm not against change. In fact, as you will see, I'm a big fan of doubling down and providing more value to customers. The key is ensuring the movement is purposeful and built on a solid foundation.

The critical distinction is deepening versus distracting. Does the change enhance your existing business and allow you to provide more value to customers? Or is it a bright, shiny object that doesn't align with what matters most?

The Third Option

Innovation is critical for any organization. Our ability to adapt, evolve, and change to meet new realities is crucial. However, these shifts should come from a position of strength that's grounded in a solid foundation. They should not be like a feather in the wind, floating aimlessly in all directions.

In today's environment of heightened competition, increased volatility, and growing uncertainty, we must establish roots that provide stability.

We often assume that only two innovation options exist: pivot or persist. Change direction or stay the course. But there is a third option that involves going deeper. The key is to identify ways to leverage what we do best to create maximum value for our customers and become critical to their success. This leads to less spinning and more winning.

> We often assume that only two innovation options exist: pivot or persist. But there is a third option that involves going deeper.

In a world where "adapt or die" has become the rallying cry, pursuing the next big thing is relentless. The promise of novel ideas, products, and technologies is intoxicating. But is pivoting for pivoting's sake the answer?

This is a moment in history when being pivotal—meaning being of crucial importance to our customers—is more vital than simply pivoting. Rather than spinning in circles, we should provide customers with a lasting and significant impact.

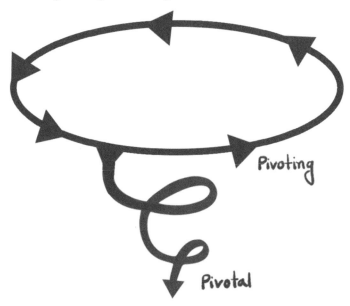

Important Definitions to Get Us Started

Before we delve further, we must agree on some definitions. Some of these may differ from what you've encountered in the past.

PIVOT: "Completely change the way in which one does something" (*Oxford English Dictionary*). "To turn or twist" (*Cambridge Dictionary*). In this book, I use the term "pivot" to describe a shift in business strategy that leads to changes in either the products or the services being offered or the way they are provided. Specifically, I argue against shifts that prevent the organization from focusing on its unique differentiator. Homejoy is a great example of a pivot gone bad. For those familiar with the lean start-up world, please note that I am not using the technical definition associated with hypothesis testing but rather with the more widely used meaning that emerged during the pandemic.

PIVOTAL: "Of crucial importance in relation to the development or success of something else" (*Oxford English Dictionary*). "Important because other things depend on it" (*Cambridge Dictionary*). It is about going deeper with customers to add more value in a way that makes you essential to them. You become irreplaceable.

DIFFERENTIATION: Contrary to traditional definitions, differentiation goes beyond merely being different, standing out, or offering unique products and services. It is the key to becoming and remaining distinctive and desirable, both now and in the foreseeable future. By leveraging your differentiator, you gain clarity on what matters most, which helps you prioritize investments and allows you to become essential to your customers, partners, and employees.

Being pivotal is about innovation that is grounded in value creation and not in the fads of the moment.

How to Use This Book

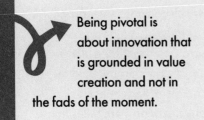

Being pivotal is about innovation that is grounded in value creation and not in the fads of the moment.

Use this book as your guide through a step-by-step process for identifying your unique differentiator and effectively utilizing it to direct your innovation investments toward achieving the highest returns while also ensuring organizational stability.

This book is divided into five primary sections:

- **Section 1. Being Pivotal Is Not About Pivoting**: We explore why changing direction too often, without first planting your feet, can lead to burnout, inefficiencies, and poor results. Here, we also start to dig deep into the concept of differentiation. We explore how to make sure you look at it through the eyes of your customers and not just your own business.
- **Section 2. Innovate Where You Differentiate**: We start with a high-level perspective on the work done within organizations. In particular, we explore the Innovation Targeting Matrix (ITM) and the three levels of capabilities: support, core, and differentiating. This is a simple yet powerful framework for creating your innovation strategy. It helps you determine where to invest in innovation and where to use other techniques. You will discover that the key mantra is "innovate where you differentiate" while using other, more efficient strategies for non-differentiating activities.
- **Section 3. The 5Ds of Differentiation**: This is a meaty section. Here we give you the tools to identify your

differentiator through five dimensions: Distinctive, Desirable, Durable, Dynamic, and Disseminated. The first four dimensions help you assess what is most important to your customers and your business—today and tomorrow. The last dimension, Disseminated, helps you create a culture of differentiation and enables you to focus your selling on what makes you special. Together, these allow you to become of pivotal importance to your customers by understanding how to create and sustain value.

- **Section 4. Beyond the Organization:** It is natural for readers to assume that the concept of differentiation is relevant only to C-suite executives and top-level management. However, this belief overlooks the true power of the tools contained in this book. When you apply the concepts of differentiation to every individual, team, and department in an organization, you unleash their full potential. For you, the reader, this section shows how to use these frameworks, whether you are an employee or entrepreneur. In addition, we explore how to apply these concepts to your personal life.

Toward the end, there are also some final thoughts that you won't want to miss, along with details of my FAST Innovation® process. FAST is an acronym that stands for the following

> Focus—Focus on differentiators.
> Ask—Ask better questions.
> Shift—Shift perspectives to reveal hidden solutions.
> Test—Test, experiment, and implement solutions.

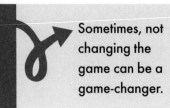

Sometimes, not changing the game can be a game-changer.

This book is the "Focus" step. It provides the critical foundation for all other work because it helps you determine the biggest opportunities—the ones you want to place the biggest bets on.

In some respects, this book is the prequel to my previous one, *Invisible Solutions: 25 Lenses that Reframe and Help Solve Difficult Business Problems*. While *Invisible Solutions* focuses on solving problems, *Pivotal* emphasizes which problems to solve.

By embracing the pivotal mindset and the power of the planted foot, you will not only unleash unprecedented clarity and value within your organization but also create an environment where employees can flourish. This book helps you determine where to double down to get the greatest returns while enabling you to make smarter and more powerful pivots when the situation requires it.

Through practical frameworks, you and your team will gain the tools and knowledge to identify your unique differentiator and effectively leverage it to direct investment of time, money, and resources.

You are pivotal. Your business is pivotal. And for you to remain pivotal, you need to know where you are now, where to dig deep, when to stay the course, and where to focus your energies to create the greatest value for others and yourself. Sometimes, not changing the game can be a game-changer.

This book is a transformative approach to innovation that provides stability in a world of constant change.

Welcome to *Pivotal*.

SECTION ONE

Know Where To Go Deep

CHAPTER 1

Being Pivotal Is Not About Pivoting

How I Went Deep in My Business

When the pandemic brought the world to a halt in March 2020, during a Zoom call I was on, a fellow keynote speaker asked me, "What are you doing to pivot your business?" With the shutdown of in-person meetings, conferences, and conventions, some aspects of my business needed to change to adapt. Part of my income was earned from appearing on stages, at training facilities, and in conference rooms.

My response caught my colleague off guard. I said, "I'm not pivoting. I'm going deep." He was confused because he assumed I would pivot to replace in-person speeches with virtual ones, like everyone else. But this is only a shift in technology rather than one of depth or value.

While the rest of the speaking industry pivoted to online, Zoom-based events, I chose to delve deeper. I asked myself, "What am I doing that creates the greatest value?" And I wondered how could I

> To be pivotal, you want to deepen relationships internally and externally, and create long-term value that makes you a strategic ally today and tomorrow.

dig deeper into that. Instead of merely converting speeches to an online platform, I focused on digging deeper—the planted foot.

To be pivotal, you want to deepen relationships internally and externally and create long-term value that makes you a strategic ally today and tomorrow.

There are things you do better than anyone else that the world craves. What are they? How can you leverage them?

In my business, for most of my post-Accenture career, I spent a significant amount of my time on stage delivering keynote speeches at large conferences for Fortune 500 companies.

Fifty speeches a year. Fifty transactions a year.

Several years ago, I realized the transactional nature of my work bothered me, not financially but existentially. Was a sixty-minute presentation genuinely making a difference? Although I know it changed how companies conducted business, I yearned for more. Creating a deep impact on an organization's outcomes and its employees became more critical than the sheer number of clients or the total amount in my bank account.

Given this realization, right before the pandemic I decided to shift from transactions to longer-term relationships. I identified what I did better than anyone else and what my clients wanted and needed, and I doubled down there. I developed programs that would transform businesses, not merely transact with them.

To achieve this outcome, I created an in-depth, apprenticeship-style mastery program, where I not only train people to master my process but also assist them in applying it and producing real-world results.

Instead of fifty transactions, I now have fewer than half a dozen deep-dive relationships, each with a transformational impact.

Depth helps my clients achieve better results. Depth allows me to focus more on relationships and less on sales. Depth creates stability.

Although adding new services that provide deeper value may seem like a pivot, I see it as doubling down on my differentiator and anchoring my business in what matters most. It's about the foot that remains stationary and provides stability. It's about being pivotal rather than transactional with my clients.

A Brief History of Pivoting

In 2020, when the world was plunged into a global pandemic, the Association of National Advertisers declared "pivot" the word of the year, reflecting the frantic efforts of organizations to adapt to a new reality. Restaurants transformed from sit-down establishments to take-out and delivery services, meetings and conferences went virtual, and travel and hospitality businesses endeavored to make planes and hotels seem safer through enhanced sanitization measures. The demand for toilet paper outstripped production as panic-buying surged. Virtually every company in every industry across the globe felt the impact.

In the context of the pandemic, a "pivot" signified any shift in business strategy. And a pivot was any change in direction, often reactionary rather than strategic.

However, the pandemic was not the sole impetus for pivoting. Factors such as out-of-control inflation, supply chain disruptions, recession worries, workforce challenges, and the rise of AI further drove businesses to pivot.

While it's easy to associate pivoting with the pandemic, the concept of adjusting one's business direction has been around for decades.

> Today there's a pervasive belief that we must "pivot or perish." But does this philosophy of constant change truly work?

In 1962, American philosopher Thomas Kuhn introduced the term "paradigm shift" in his book *The Structure of Scientific Revolutions*. This term described how companies or industries adapted to evolving market conditions, shifting consumer preferences, technological innovations, and competitive pressures—a concept that undoubtedly resonates today.

In 2009, Eric Ries, author of the best-selling book *The Lean Startup*, expanded upon this idea by incorporating the term "pivot" into the business vocabulary. Ries defined a pivot as "a structured course correction designed to test a new fundamental hypothesis about the product, strategy, and engine of growth." In essence, this approach involved testing hypotheses to ensure that a potential product aligned with market needs.

Although the concept of pivoting was primarily applied to agile start-ups and product launches, it has since permeated the broader business world and has come to represent any shift in direction.

And today there's a pervasive belief that we must "pivot or perish." But does this philosophy of constant change truly work?

Undoubtedly, there are instances when pivoting is essential. One need only look at the examples of Blockbuster, BlackBerry, or Sears to understand that a failure to change direction can be disastrous. However, pivoting from a position of instability may also result in squandered energy and resources.

Although Kuhn is frequently cited by others who support the "change or die" mentality, he viewed a paradigm shift as a last resort to be undertaken only in response to a profound crisis. The smartphone represented a significant crisis for BlackBerry. Similarly, pivoting during the pandemic was a necessary step for many organizations. But does this mean we should be in a constant state of flux? Perhaps not.

Peter Thiel, cofounder of PayPal and numerous other start-ups said, "I'm personally quite skeptical of all the lean start-up methodology. I think the really great companies did something that was somewhat more of a quantum improvement that really differentiated them from everybody else."

Being differentiated is the name of the game. And doubling down on your differentiator is the way to win that game.

If you are a small start-up with untested hypotheses, there is value in validating your assumptions through pivoting. This allows you to get insights from the market before investing heavily. However, if you're a more established organization with a history of data, relationships, and experience, the reactive nature of continual pivoting may cause you to take frequent and potentially dangerous detours. It can also be destructive to your organization.

> Being differentiated is the name of the game. And doubling down on your differentiator is the way to win that game.

A 2019 study by Prosci found that 73 percent of organizations reported being past or nearing the saturation point. Only 8 percent said that their organization had plenty of spare capacity for change. Overload seems to be the norm.

What if nonstop pivoting dissipates and saps your energy because you become enamored with too many distractions? What if continued shifting of direction confuses and burns out your employees? What if constantly changing course annoys your customers because they don't feel any level of stability in what you offer? What if all this shifting makes you seem unreliable to your partners and vendors?

It seems as though today everyone is pivoting, spinning around in circles, and getting dizzy. But it doesn't have to be this way. And it shouldn't be this way. It causes too much damage.

The Non-Financial Cost of Change

Change overload is not new. According to a 2013 PwC survey of more than two thousand executives, managers, and employees, 65 percent reported change fatigue, while only about half felt their organization had the ability to deliver the changes.

To make matters worse, 44 percent of the employees said they didn't understand the change they were being asked to make, while 38 percent didn't agree with what they did understand. Confusion and disagreement lead to disengagement. And remember, this study was done before the pandemic, before all hell broke loose and pivoting became the norm.

Imagine you're working for a company (hint: you probably are) that gives you ambiguous, conflicting, or changing directions, *and* you don't agree with everything you hear. Does this make you happy and productive? I suspect not.

The solution to this nonstop direction shifting is depth—depth of value, relationships, and competency. It is about building trust. Sometimes we're to blame for inadvertently fracturing trust by valuing the new over the now. Depth is the opposite of going after the flavor of the month.

> A 2019 study by Prosci found that 73 percent of organizations reported being past or nearing the saturation point. Only 8 percent said that their organization had plenty of spare capacity for change. Overload is the norm.

This is a moment in history when depth and nurturing trust have taken center stage. A more recent PwC survey conducted in 2023 revealed that a staggering 91 percent of business executives agree that cultivating and sustaining trust has a direct, positive impact on their financial performance. But here's the intriguing twist: while a confident 84 percent of these executives believe their customers hold their company in high trust, a mere 27 percent of customers actually do. This striking disparity unveils a captivating challenge for businesses in today's rapidly evolving world—bridging the trust gap by fostering deeper, more meaningful relationships with customers. It's about being in it for the long haul and understanding long-term implications. It's about being shoulder to shoulder with your customers, employees, and partners.

This is a moment in history when depth and nurturing trust have taken center stage.

This deepening approach is a decision-making strategy for investing in the areas of your business that will have the greatest impact. It's about purposeful change built on a solid foundation. It's about the planted foot.

It's about purposeful change built on a solid foundation. It's about the planted foot.

To Delve Deep, Identify What to Stop Doing

Going deeper doesn't necessarily mean adding products and services. Often, it means knowing what to stop doing to achieve clarity of focus. In doing so, you can better serve your customers.

Knowing what to kill isn't easy because we have emotional attachments to our work. Plus, the "sunk costs" associated with past investments may make it tempting to continue investing.

But sticking with something just because you have done it in the past is a terrible investment. Holding onto something that is declining can sap the entire organization's energy. In gardening, you prune dying branches of a tree to conserve valuable resources for the healthy parts of the plant.

This doesn't mean pivoting. Going deep often can occur when you prune away whatever is not serving your best purpose.

Steve Jobs went deep at Apple when he returned to the company in 1997. Instead of identifying more products to create, he simplified the line-up down to only four products: iMac, Power Mac, iBook, and PowerBook. Apple reduced the product line by 70 percent. This simplified the company's operations, allowing it to focus on its core strengths. It streamlined its manufacturing and distribution processes, thus reducing costs while improving profitability. Additionally, by focusing on a smaller number of products, Apple was able to concentrate its marketing and advertising efforts, making it easier to create a cohesive brand message. They also went deep on design as a differentiator. This had a transformative impact on the company. Apple was able to turn a profit in 1998 after losing $1.04 billion the year before. Of course, over time they added new products as the company grew and their resources were able to handle the added work.

> Going deeper doesn't necessarily mean adding products and services. Often, it means knowing what to stop doing and where to double down.

Sometimes what looks like a pivot is a company going deep. In 2005, IBM famously exited the consumer hardware market when they sold the ThinkPad line to Lenovo. On the surface, it looked like they were changing the direction of the company, but in fact they were doubling down on the areas of the business that were paying the greatest dividends: enterprise services and solutions. These had higher margins and greater growth potential. The PC market, on the other hand, was becoming increasingly commoditized and competitive with lower profit margins. The divestiture allowed IBM to avoid the distraction of the PC business. Plus, the partnership with Lenovo further enhanced IBM's reach into the enterprise space. It wasn't about something new but a clarification about what matters most. To further narrow its focus, in 2021 the company split off its managed infrastructure services business. This allowed IBM to continue deepening its work in consulting, cloud, AI, and other high-profit and high-value areas.

> Antoine de Saint-Exupéry, author of *The Little Prince*, once said, "Perfection is finally attained not when there is no longer anything to add but when there is no longer anything to take away."

Knowing what to stop doing and where to double down is key to going deep. It helps the planted foot get even deeper. Although pivoting and shifting may capture the imagination, innovation is about impact, making a difference. Constantly changing direction dissipates energies and impact. Killing off something is not the same as pivoting. Removing what is not working is so important.

I love the quote from Antoine de Saint-Exupéry, author of *The Little Prince*, who once said, "Perfection is finally attained not when there is no longer anything to add but when there is no longer anything to take away." This beautifully sums up how to get a better differentiator by knowing what to eliminate. If your differentiator is about going deep, prune away whatever prevents that.

Being pivotal means knowing where to go deep.

Solve Deeper Problems for Your Best Customers

An exercise I do with my clients involves asking them to consider solutions to the question, "How can we get more *customers*?" The answers are predictable: marketing, advertising, social media, cold calling, and referrals. The goal of getting more customers is either to get people who don't know you to become aware of your existence or to get people who know of you to do business with you. This is often a difficult strategy to execute.

Next, I ask the audience to provide solutions to a slightly different question: "How can we get more *revenue*?" Notice that we changed only one word in the question, but now we unleash a wide range of new and different solutions. Yes, getting more customers might be one answer. Raising pricing might be another. But a potentially more powerful solution is to sell more to existing customers. This avoids the difficult—and often more expensive—task of attracting new prospects.

I argue this is done by creating more value for them. When you solve your customer's problems, they will see value in paying for the product or service. To do this, either solve a wider range of their problems or solve bigger problems. Both will lead to increased revenues. The key is to make sure you are always leveraging your strengths rather than moving in a different direction. You can increase revenues through the depth of relationships without requiring more customers.

> Going deep doesn't mean drilling in a thousand different places. Being pivotal means knowing where to drill.

But as we learned from the Homejoy example, you need to make sure this is built on a solid foundation of your differentiator.

Finally, I have the audience consider another reframe: "How can we get more *profits*?" Again, we changed just one word in the question, but we now get a very different range of answers. In my experience, our least-profitable customers are the ones who are the highest maintenance. Therefore, a good solution might be to stop doing business with your least-profitable customers and focus instead on those you can make the greatest impact on.

Here's what's fascinating: we started with the assumption that we wanted more customers. But with a simple change of a couple of words, we ended up preferring fewer, yet more profitable customers—deeper relationships with the customers whom we can best serve. Get rid of anything—products, services, customers—that doesn't serve you in going deep and delivering the greatest value possible. Instead of trying to do more with less (which stretches people thin), you can do less and get more. Fewer yet more profitable customers. Deeper relationships.

This leads us to where *you* should go deep. What problems do you solve? Can you solve a wider range of problems for your existing and best customers? Can you go deeper with them? Can you solve bigger and more important problems?

This simple line of questioning might help you stop spinning and start focusing. Changing the questions you ask will have a profound impact on the solutions you see. But too often we jump to solutions—sometimes pivoting to new ideas—without taking the time to consider if this shift is appropriate.

This process of changing your questions to reveal different solutions is called reframing. And this is what I did to go deeper with my business.

Reframing for Depth

At the beginning of this chapter, I shared how I went deeper with my clients by moving from transactions to transformation. But this wasn't the first time I doubled down on my differentiator. Even before that program-level decision, I went deeper with my content.

Best Practices Are Stupid: 40 Ways to Out-Innovate the Competition was a broad-brush approach into the world of innovation. It focused on forty different tips for making innovation a reality, ranging from strategy and measures to process, organization, and technology.

One of the chapters that piqued readers' interest focused on the idea that asking better questions (a.k.a. reframing) can lead to more innovative solutions. In this chapter, the importance of improving the quality of the questions asked by innovators is explored. I remember one review of the book which said, "Love the chapter on reframing! But unfortunately, you only tell us why it is important and what to do. You don't address the all-important topic of how to actually do it. Can you write a book just on that one topic?"

I thought this was a great idea, although it took a decade to write the actual book. In the months following the publication of *Best Practices Are Stupid*, I set out to develop a systematic method for reframing and asking better questions. The idea was to catalog "lenses" that could help people see problems from different perspectives. Over the course of a couple of years, I created a spreadsheet that contained more than one hundred lenses. I used these with clients during workshops and consulting engagements. The results were amazing. Companies found solutions to problems they had never considered. In some cases, problems that couldn't be solved in years were solved in minutes.

> What problems do you solve? Can you solve a wider range of problems for your existing and best customers? Can you go deeper with them? Can you solve bigger and more important problems?

After ten years of populating the spreadsheet and using the lenses with clients, I decided it was finally time to turn the list into a book. That is when *Invisible Solutions* was born. I found the twenty-five most widely used lenses and pulled them together into a full-length book.

I discovered that when done correctly, going deep can expand your business as you go narrower. It allows you to add more value for your current customers so that they want to extend their business relationship with you.

> When done correctly, going deep by focusing more narrowly can expand your business. It allows you to add more value for your current customers, encouraging them to extend their business relationship with you.

How You Can Go Deep in Your Business

This book has one simple purpose: to help you figure out where, when, and how to go deep.

Depth is crucial to being pivotal. Rather than just transacting with your customers and clients, you gain a thorough understanding of their pains and provide unique solutions that only you can offer. Once you determine where to go deep, you can leverage this to prioritize your investments, helping you figure out where to place your bets. It will give you clarity in a way you've most likely never had before. One key to this is to determine your differentiator.

Your differentiator isn't what makes you different. It's why someone will do business with you and only you. It's the most important part of your business and is where you go deep. To be clear, it is not a department or function. Every person in your organization contributes to your differentiator.

Getting clarity on where to go deep will enable you to laser-focus your energies rather than dissipate them. It is a powerful tool that helps

> Your differentiator isn't what makes you different. It's why someone will do business with you and only you. It's the most important part of your business and is where you go deep.

you determine where to innovate and when to use other strategies. This clarity gives your entire organization a clear sense of purpose, maximizing the impact of their efforts.

When you master this process, you and your organization will have the confidence needed to take your business in the right direction.

It's time to become pivotal.

CHAPTER 2

Let's Get Pivotal

What Is Most Important to Your Organization?

A challenge for many organizations is to know when to pivot and when to stick with it. It's not always obvious where to focus on change and where to plant your feet. But getting it wrong could mean spinning in circles or, even worse, destroying something that has traditionally been of great value to the organization. This is an issue that would keep executives up at night if they only knew the impact.

I remember a meeting with a client team that was struggling to prioritize their investments. They asked me to give them an example of how others go through the process. I decided to try a thought experiment with them. I asked them to imagine that

> A challenge for many organizations is knowing when to pivot and when to stick with it.

they worked in the property and casualty insurance industry, which offers insurance for cars, homes, and similar items.

To get them started, I gave them a list of some common processes for the insurance industry: Develop Products and Services, Customer Service, Manage Revenues, Manage Distribution Channels, Market Products and Services, Underwriting, Claims Fulfillment, Manage the Provider Network, and Plan and Manage the Enterprise.

When you look at this list, which do you think is most important? Without having any other information, what does your gut tell you would be the place to target your innovation investments? I asked the group, "What is the most important process to an insurance company?" In other words, if you worked in this industry, where should you invest the most money?

The first response from my client group was "Claims Fulfillment." "Why?" I asked, and they said, "Because this is why customers get insurance in the first place." This made sense, as customers buy insurance so that when they have a claim to file, they will get paid promptly. I responded, "Claims Fulfillment is indeed a very important process. But it is not *the* most important one."

Someone else then suggested Manage Revenues. Why? "Because this is how the company makes money," was their response. Again, I commended the person for their answer but let them know that it was still not the most important part of the business.

This continued for a while until nearly every process has been suggested. Some people then hedged their bets and said, "All of them." Nope. If you try to be the best at everything, you'll be great at nothing. The final attempt was, "None of them." It was a clever response, but it still wasn't correct. At this point I stopped the group and said, "The answer is two words: it depends."

It Depends

There is no universal part of any business that is most important. Every company in every industry should respond to this question differently. This is your competitive advantage. Unless you are already the market leader, if your differentiator is the same as the competition, that could be an issue.

Consider four insurance companies serving relatively similar markets.

State Farm: Competitive positioning for State Farm depends on its exclusive (and extensive) network of agents and offices. Its wide geographic coverage is reinforced by the company's motto: "Like a good neighbor, State Farm is there." The firm differentiates itself from the rest of the pack through this slogan and network. In an age when most companies have replaced the human touch with internet-based services, having a local, personal presence nearly everywhere has secured State Farm's position as the largest insurance company. They've captured 10 percent of the overall property and

There is no universal part of any business that is most important.

casualty market, 18 percent of the automotive insurance premiums, and 21 percent of the home insurance market. Pervasiveness is their path to profit.

USAA: While State Farm relies on geographic coverage, this would not work for USAA. Their customers are members of the military and their families. Given the potentially transient nature of their target market, USAA's business model transcends geography. For example, they were the first to develop technologies that allow members to deposit checks from their cell phones—a convenience for those serving overseas or far from a bank. To better understand their members, they hire extensively from the military community and offer free financial advice to those who are being deployed or returning to civilian life. And its Survivor Relations team helps family members cope with the death of a loved one. The company's mantra is "Serving Those Who Serve." With this focus, year after year, USAA has ranked number one or two in terms of customer service when measured against any company across all industries. Each year USAA retains 98 percent of its members, and 92 percent say they will never leave.

PURE: Their target community is high-net-worth families. Given this, they provide an extraordinary level of service. This is evidenced by a story they shared with me. A family experienced a fire in their living room. Sadly, it was during Christmastime and destroyed everything, including sentimental keepsakes the parents had collected during their travels. Unlike other insurance companies that might give the policyholder a check and say, "Good luck!," PURE temporarily relocated the family to a home comparable to their own. The company then restored their home to its original condition by hiring contractors and managing the entire process. The amazing part is that PURE agents studied the pictures the family had of their collectibles, and they searched the internet to find replacements. The goal was for the family to move back into their home with everything the way it was before the fire.

Lemonade: Founded in 2015, Lemonade is almost the exact opposite of State Farm. They are primarily a technology company with no local agents. Pretty much all business is conducted online, including quotes, purchases, claims, and bill paying. Their model is also somewhat different. According to their website, "Lemonade reverses the

> Within an industry, capabilities that are differentiating for one organization may be less critical for another.

traditional insurance model. We treat the premiums you pay as if it's your money, not ours. With Lemonade, everything becomes simple and transparent. We take a flat fee, pay claims super fast, and give back what's left to causes you care about." They are a certified B Corp, which means they give back to the community.

What is the most important capability for State Farm? Its distribution network is crucial because it serves a wide segment of the population by offering local support. On the other hand, USAA is focused on customer service for the military, regardless of geography. For PURE, one source of differentiation is exceptional claims fulfillment for high-net-worth families. And lastly, Lemonade differentiates itself on technology and its B Corp business model.

The point is that capabilities that are differentiating for one organization may well be less critical for another in the same industry. All four of these companies are in similar businesses, but each concentrates on a different aspect to achieve a competitive advantage in the marketplace.

Although the examples above might seem simplistic, they make an important point: to maximize your investments, you need to determine what's most important to your business. In other words, innovate where you differentiate. Find and leverage your differentiator to go deep—a deeper connection to your roots and a deeper connection to your customers' needs. This is the area of your business that will yield the greatest returns. This is the planted foot and is key to how you become pivotal.

> To maximize your investments, you need to determine what's most important to your business. In other words, innovate where you differentiate.

And to determine what matters most to your organization, you must first determine what is most important to your customers.

Differentiation Is Not a Product or Service

Why do customers flock to you and not someone else? What makes you special? What separates you from the competition? It's not about specific products or services but rather the capabilities you possess that create value for your customers. It's a sustainable engine that keeps you competitive over a long period of time. It's the stability your organization needs to limit constant shifting.

When seeking stability, look no further than Radio Flyer. Established in 1917, the company is renowned for its iconic "The Original Little Red Wagon." Over the years, Radio Flyer has diversified its product line to include tricycles and scooters. However, it's not the products that make the company special, especially given the presence of many lower-cost competitors. Their differentiator lies in their focus on high-quality products that evoke a sense of American nostalgia. It's a wholesome company with strong roots.

Robert Pasin, the current CEO and grandson of the company's original founder, is so passionate about Radio Flyer that he's affectionately known as the Chief Wagon Officer. In defining their differentiator, he emphasized emotion over products. He shared with me, "I ask our customers, and almost everyone I meet, questions that focus on the brand rather than the product. What does Radio Flyer mean to people? What emotions does it evoke? How do people describe their experiences with it?

"Some strong themes emerged. Usually, the first thing people do when they hear 'Radio Flyer' is smile. The next thing they do is share a story. Stories about their wagon being a race car, a rocket, a

> Why do customers choose you over others? What sets you apart from the competition? It's not just your products or services, but the unique capabilities you offer that create value for your customers.

spaceship, a submarine, a motorboat, or a magic carpet. Listening to these stories, I encountered themes of outdoor play, sunshine, green grass, wind-blown hair, laughter, love, and cherished memories.

"Given this feedback, we articulated our purpose: Radio Flyer exists to 'bring smiles and create warm memories that last a lifetime.' That encapsulates what our brand means to people. We transitioned from making wagons to fostering smiles and cherished memories. This realization gave us a broader and more exhilarating purpose, marking a pivotal mindset shift that spurred our growth."

They sell a feeling, not just a product. And that feeling is irreplaceable. No one else can replicate it. It is the ultimate differentiator.

Customers adore Radio Flyer, and the sentiment is shared by its employees. In 2015, *Fortune* ranked Radio Flyer as the top small business to work for. In a move that further underscores its commitment, it became a Certified B Corporation in September 2022, standing out as the first global toy manufacturer recognized for its dedication to positive environmental and social impact.

Tiffany & Co. has a similar emotional differentiator. Yes, they have beautiful jewelry. But what makes them special is the feeling one gets when receiving a gift in the famous Tiffany Blue® box. When searching for your differentiator, look beyond just products and services, and be sure to tap into emotions.

Identifying what's most important isn't as simple as what I described in the insurance industry examples. To complicate matters, most organizations need to excel in multiple areas, and what is important today may not be as important tomorrow (see the "dynamic"

> Radio Flyer sells a feeling, not just a product. And that feeling is irreplaceable. No one else can replicate it. It is the ultimate differentiator.

section for more on this). Although your differentiation may not immediately be obvious, with the frameworks in this book, you can get clarity on what matters most.

What's Your Differentiator?

In its simplest form, your differentiator is the reason someone does business with you and not someone else. But there is much more to it than that. Being distinctive (the "different" in differentiated) is only one of five dimensions to consider when defining your differentiator. Being different for the sake of being different is not the same as being differentiated. Differentiation is a way to create lasting relevance.

Zappos has been known as a company with an exceptional culture that drives incredible customer service. They have differentiated themselves in the online retail industry by offering free shipping and returns, a 365-day return policy, and a commitment to going above and beyond for their customers.

Amazon, now the owner of Zappos, has an incredible warehousing and logistics network. They can cost-effectively ship products pretty much anywhere in the world, creating a capability that is difficult to duplicate.

Patagonia has differentiated itself in the outdoor apparel industry by its commitment to sustainability and environmental activism. Their focus on using environmentally friendly materials and supporting conservation efforts has helped them build a loyal customer base that values their commitment to social responsibility. Their Worn Wear

> In its simplest form, your differentiator is the reason someone does business with you and not someone else. But there is much more to it than that. Differentiation is a way to create lasting relevance.

program encourages customers to repair and reuse their clothing instead of buying new items. Also, they have invested in organic cotton farming and launched a line of recycled polyester clothing made from post-consumer waste.

Note that none of these companies differentiate on a specific product. Zappos sells the same shoes as everyone else. Amazon sells pretty much everything. And the same goes for Patagonia, which focuses primarily on sustainability and social responsibility.

Your differentiator will be a powerful tool for helping you identify opportunities and prioritize investments. It will help you focus precisely on what matters most, rather than chase every opportunity.

It will help you become and stay pivotal.

SECTION TWO

Innovate Where You Differentiate

CHAPTER 3

The Three Levels of Capabilities

Everyone Contributes to Your Differentiator

Field agents at a major insurance company valued their ability to provide a single point of contact to their customers. It was an admirable goal. Unfortunately, it led to political battles without any way to deal with them.

The issue was with the claims experts who were called in to solve the most difficult claims. Inside the company, this group was treated as a back-office function. As a result, it was assumed that they should never interact with the customer.

While looking at the business and department through the lens of differentiation, they had an epiphany. Although the claims group was viewed as a cost center, it was indeed performing many differentiating capabilities. This was the source of animosity between the claims experts and field offices.

> Your differentiator is not a department, function, or role. Every person in every department can and should contribute to your differentiator.

Inside the organization, every time one of the claims experts "overstepped" their bounds by moving into a client-facing, differentiating role, the field offices felt threatened. The people who felt accountable for bringing in money and serving the customer generally didn't want the back-office, cost-center people telling them how to do it. They didn't mind support, but generally, they wanted to be left to themselves when determining these types of critical interactions.

The company has always considered its ability to handle claims quickly and efficiently to be one of its key differentiators. Plus, they pride themselves on their ability to pay customers exactly what they are entitled to receive. No cutting corners. That even translated to agents informing customers of policy benefits they were unaware of. At the same time, they wanted to make sure that they didn't overpay. Doing so would hurt customers, as it would result in premium increases across the board. Given this, the goal was to always hit the bull's-eye, paying out exactly what was due—no more, no less.

For all of these reasons, claims is an incredibly important differentiator. Although in the past they assumed it was only the field agent's responsibility, they now see the power and value of having the claims experts directly handle claims when the field agent is not available. This is not a pivot. This is going deeper into what makes sense for the customer, with fast and efficient claims processing being critical. This is an insight that they probably would not have reached had they not looked at the activities performed by different roles.

By focusing on customer needs instead of engaging in internal turf battles, the two departments discovered how they could each be pivotal. They learned how to leverage their unique strengths to create the most efficient claims process.

This illustrates several important points as it relates to differentiation.

First, your differentiator is not a department, function, or role. Every person in every department can and should contribute to your differentiator. What's equally important, your differentiator is not a product, service, or offering. It is a set of capabilities that helps you distinguish yourself in a crowded market and that will stand the test of time.

> Your differentiator is not a product, service, or offering. It is a set of capabilities that helps you distinguish yourself in a crowded market and that will stand the test of time.

In his book *Animal Farm*, George Orwell writes, "All animals are equal, but some animals are more equal than others." In business, all capabilities are important, but some are more important than others. Not all capabilities are differentiating, and therefore not all should be treated the same. There are three levels of capabilities: support, core, and differentiating. The goal is to innovate where you differentiate and to use different strategies for support and core.

The Three Levels of Capabilities

Let's dig into each of the three levels.

Support

Support capabilities are those that are necessary for running the business, yet they do not create direct customer value. Sometimes people make the mistake of assuming departments like Human Resources, Information Technology, or Finance are support functions. They are not! There are no support functions, only support activities.

> Peter Drucker once said, "There is nothing so useless as doing efficiently that which should not be done at all."

Yes, people in these departments do some work that is support in nature. But they also do work that is core and differentiating. These three levels do not represent functions, departments, roles, individuals, or even teams. They are activities and capabilities. Every person in every department does a combination of support, core, and differentiating. When done correctly, every person understands how they contribute to the organization's differentiator.

Strategies for Support Capabilities: Because support capabilities do not create external value, you ideally want to find ways to eliminate, minimize, delegate, or outsource this work. Your goal is to keep costs to a minimum and avoid having this work be a distraction. Regardless, it needs to be high quality.

A simple example is payroll. Unless you are in the payroll business, like ADP, investing in developing the world's best payroll system makes no sense. You would be wasting valuable time and money that could be invested in customer-facing work. Therefore, outsourcing to a third party is a great strategy.

But always remember, you should first look to see what can be eliminated. As Peter Drucker once said, "There is nothing so useless as doing efficiently that which should not be done at all." Check your assumptions. Do you really need to do this work? What would happen if you stopped?

For many organizations, meetings are support, and I would argue that many should be eliminated. Time tracking has been a staple for running a business. But do we really need to know down to the last minute where time is spent? Probably not. If you do, is there a more efficient and cost-effective way to achieve the result? What is the cost of having people spend their time tracking their time? Or what are the negative consequences of having people who don't accurately track their time attempt to rewrite history and justify how they should have spent their time? This is unproductive and not useful for anyone involved.

You may read this section on support and think that the concept is relatively straightforward. Although it might seem obvious, many of my clients are investing too heavily in support. However, it becomes particularly interesting when you fold in the next two levels.

Core

Core activities are critical to your business but are not your source of competitive advantage. Although these create direct value for the customer, they are (to use a gambling term) only table stakes. They are the cost of entry. They are not the reason someone will do business with you. But if you get them wrong, it might be a reason someone leaves.

The planted foot is so critical here, as your core is a foundation on which everything else is built. For a manufacturing company, core activities might include order fulfillment, order acquisition, and product support. Quite often, these capabilities can be "transactional" in nature. They are foundational, yet not differentiating.

Strategies for Core Capabilities: Core work needs to be a well-oiled machine—cost-effective with high levels of quality. Errors can't be tolerated.

> Core activities are crucial to your business but don't define your competitive edge. They're akin to table stakes in gambling—necessary for entry but not a unique draw for customers. While getting them right won't necessarily win business, getting them wrong might drive customers away.

Although you don't have to be the best at it, you need to be great. Therefore, your primary strategies are to simplify (potentially using lean or Six Sigma techniques), automate, develop strategic partnerships, or use proven practices.

An example of core in action can be seen in a company called CCC. In the automotive insurance industry, most insurance companies have decided that the technology behind claims processing is not differentiating but is core. Investing in developing an in-house system would be overkill.

However, it is differentiating to CCC, the company that provides these services to most of the big insurance companies. CCC is in over 25,000 of the 40,000 collision repairers in place today. And they received a boost in December 2020 when State Farm said it would require all select service shops to use CCC effective April 1, 2021.

Support and core capabilities are critical because they form the foundation of your business differentiators. It is important that they operate at a high level of efficiency. However, it is not where you should focus your primary efforts. Instead, consider cost-effective strategies to ensure that these capabilities are operating optimally.

This leads us, finally, to differentiating capabilities.

Differentiating

Differentiating capabilities are those that set you apart from your competition. They are the reason someone chooses to do business with you and not someone else. These are your most important capabilities and require the most attention. Ideally, you have only a few of these capabilities, as you can't be great at everything. Target what is most important and laser focus there. We'll get deeper into the definition of your differentiator later in the rest of the book. But let's handle some important basics first.

Strategies for Differentiating: Differentiating work is where you want to make the greatest investment. Because this is what your customers value most about you, make sure you get this right and continue to double down in these areas. Ideally, you want to empower workers to deliver non-cookie-cutter results that will continually set you apart from your competitors.

> Differentiating capabilities are those that set you apart from your competition. They are the reason someone chooses to do business with you and not someone else.

Your main strategy is to use novel and innovative techniques to arrive at unique solutions, hence the expression "innovate where you differentiate." To repeat (as it is so important), a differentiator is not a job, role, person, department, or function. Everyone contributes to your differentiation.

And everyone contributes to innovation. While not every individual may be directly involved in creating new products or services, they are constantly seeking solutions to significant problems and opportunities. Innovation is the process of generating greater value for customers to ensure your continued relevance. Everyone is pivotal to your organization's success.

While focusing on differentiators is a priority, don't immediately invest solely in them. First, ensure that your core is optimized and grounded. Otherwise, chasing differentiators may leave you spinning in circles.

Make Sure Your Core Is Working

A software company I know was at the pinnacle of its industry, boasting an impressive suite of products and an ever-growing list of satisfied customers. It appeared to have everything going for it. However, this isn't a story of continued success and ascent to greater heights. No, this is a story of ambition, distraction, and the dangerous allure of bright, shiny objects.

The company's leaders, like most visionaries, were always looking for ways to improve and innovate. They believed in the power of listening to their customers. As the team diligently gathered input, they found that while some desired features aligned with their core product, many were completely off the beaten path.

The leaders faced a crucial crossroads: Should they stay focused on their core product or embrace these new and exciting possibilities? Although it shouldn't have been an either/or decision, they became enamored of the prospect of expanding their empire. To do this, they embarked on an acquisition spree, snapping up smaller companies in a feverish attempt to round out their offerings and cater to customer requests.

Unfortunately, the leaders had fallen prey to the seductive allure of diversification and world domination. And they lost sight of what had propelled them to their initial success: their core product.

While the company focused on acquisitions, the main software began to languish, growing increasingly outdated and becoming unable to address mounting customer concerns. In addition, critical business functions like contracting, onboarding, and training were left unattended, causing once-loyal clients to grow disillusioned.

Despite their interest in the company's new capabilities, customers were driven away by the poor state of the core product they once loved. They left in droves, their trust shattered, and the likelihood of them returning to the software vendor was slim to none.

> Even the most successful companies can fall victim to the novelty trap. Sometimes, in the pursuit of the new, we risk losing the very thing that made us great in the first place.

This story is a reminder of how even the most successful companies can fall victim to the novelty trap. Sometimes, in the pursuit of the new, we risk losing the very thing that made us great in the first place.

Before you start worrying about innovation and differentiation, ensure your "core" is working well and is optimized for efficiency with low error rates and high service levels. Not doing this is a mistake.

There's nothing worse than having a fantastic product with poor delivery or a highly desirable service that is inconsistent. The world is littered with great ideas, innovations, and businesses that were poorly executed. Invest in getting your core working perfectly before trying to improve your differentiator.

Once your core is solid, then you can double down on differentiation. One way to achieve this is by tapping into the power of specialization, allowing each individual to focus on their unique source of differentiation. In the realm of drug discovery, this concept proved especially impactful.

> There's nothing worse than having a fantastic product with poor delivery or a highly desirable service that is inconsistent.

The Power of Specialization

In the heart of a thriving pharmaceutical company, a dilemma was brewing. Tens of thousands of drug candidates were synthesized each year, but the process of purifying these compounds was proving to be a significant challenge. For those unfamiliar with the term, "drug candidates" are potential medicines undergoing evaluation for their safety and efficacy before becoming approved.

The chemists, who were the backbone of the company's innovation, found themselves mired in the cumbersome task of purifying

> When people can focus on what they do best (their personal differentiator), they can excel and produce exceptional results.

these drug candidates. Purifying drugs is a critical process that ensures the removal of impurities and unwanted byproducts, ultimately resulting in a pure and potent compound ready for further testing and development. Unfortunately, this task was not their forte, leaving ample room for improvement.

Day by day, these skilled chemists found themselves dedicating valuable time to drug purification, detracting from their primary function of designing and creating new drug candidates. It was evident that their unique talents were being underutilized. Recognizing the problem, the company decided to take a bold step. They created a dedicated team of specialists whose sole responsibility was to purify the vast pool of drug candidates. This team, equipped with knowledge and expertise in purification techniques, embraced the challenge with enthusiasm.

The transformation was remarkable. With the burden of purification lifted, the chemists could once again devote their time and energy to their true passion: designing and synthesizing novel drug candidates. Their productivity soared by at least 40 percent, while the company's purification labor costs dropped by an impressive 60 percent. By enabling individuals to concentrate on their areas of expertise, the company was able to increase efficiency, reduce costs, and ultimately accelerate the drug discovery process.

This story is a perfect example of specialization and differentiation. When people can focus on what they do best (their personal differentiator), they can excel and produce exceptional results. And in the world of drug discovery, where every moment counts, this can make all the difference.

When done correctly, every person in your organization contributes to your differentiator. When done incorrectly, some people might feel marginalized. They might feel they are not valuable if their work is not viewed as helping the company stand out. Therefore, it is crucial that people see their impact and contribution to the organization's differentiator. (Read the "disseminated internally" section to learn how to ensure everyone understands, aligns with, and operationalizes your differentiator.)

CHAPTER 4

The Innovation Targeting Matrix

Use the Right Strategy for the Right Capability

Let's pull it all together in a simple framework I call the Innovation Targeting Matrix (ITM). I've used this model (with some modifications) for over twenty years. It is one of my most powerful frameworks, as it helps organizations identify the right strategies for everything in their business.

The left column represents the level of capability: support, core, and differentiating. The middle column is the strategy to be used, and the right column is the overall goal. Keep the chart handy. It's simple, but it can have a profound impact on the way you prioritize your investments.

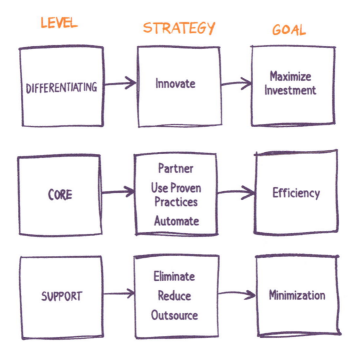

Use Your Differentiator Everywhere

The ITM is valuable not only at the enterprise level but also within each team or department.

During my Accenture days, I was actively involved in training other consultants on process and innovation methodologies. We were spending millions of dollars developing expensive training programs, yet we never really knew if we were getting the biggest bang for our buck. Traditionally, a "gut feel" strategy had been used to determine where training dollars were spent.

> The ITM is valuable not only at the enterprise level but also with each individual, team, or department.

Given this problem, a colleague of mine, Brad Kolar, decided to use the ITM within our training organization. This enabled them to reevaluate the curriculum and ensure investments were focused on getting the greatest value for money.

For training, we modified the terms slightly to fit our needs. "Differentiating" skills (and the associated training programs) were those necessary to beat the competition. These represented our special sauce. "Core" consulting skills created great value but were not unique to us. And "support" meant that the skill was commonplace and that it *enabled* the delivery.

The goal was to match the investment to the value it provided. The strategies for training and development included the following:

- Support: Completely outsource, leveraging public-domain and off-the-shelf training modules. This required less investment and, more importantly, limited time and resources.
- Core: Design and partner with world-class training organizations to provide tailored versions of existing training.

- Differentiating: Design, build, and deliver high-value proprietary courses in-house with the help of internal thought leaders.

> While many might view training as support in nature, like all functions, it encompasses activities from all three levels. Equally, functions that might appear to be differentiating will have support and core activities.

When the training courses were mapped on the ITM, everyone quickly realized that most of the investment money and resources had typically gone to the internal development of lower-value public domain knowledge training, often targeting thousands of newer hires or younger consultants. Sometimes, as in this case, it is easy to confuse volume with value. These fundamental courses were important but not a primary source of value. Therefore, instead of custom building training for basic programming and functional skills, we outsourced most of that to a third party that had vast libraries of videos on the topics. In addition to providing huge cost savings, it let us devote our internal resources to programs of higher, unique value, such as courses that relied on proprietary content.

These high-value courses were created by a small group of experts in their spare time. Because these skills were rarer, it was difficult to tap into these resources to build the training. But developing quality courses was critical, as this is where differentiating value was derived. Because there were typically no externally available options for these specialized topics, the solution was to partner the content experts with instructional designers. This allowed the experts to narrowly focus on their area of specialization while leveraging others to create the courses.

As you can imagine, the insight brought forth by this analysis rapidly shifted investments, and the appropriate strategies were used for each training course.

While many might view training as support in nature, like all functions, it encompasses activities from all three levels. Equally, functions that

> What is differentiating today for one organization might only be core for another. Each company will have a unique combination.

might appear to be differentiating—such as sales—will have support and core activities. How much time do important sales teams spend on selling? By my estimate, on average, under 30 percent. The rest of the time is spent on support and core work such as travel, time tracking, meetings, paperwork, dealing with internal bureaucracy, and more. Instead, if you can get them working on what's most important, they will add even more value to the organization. For anything that is not sales, either eliminate it or have someone else take that work off their plate.

Again, what is differentiating for one organization might only be core for another. Each company will have a unique combination. That's what makes the process so difficult—and fun. There is not a cookie-cutter, one-size-fits-all strategy.

Remember that insurance company at the beginning of this chapter—the one with the turf wars? The ITM was the tool that helped them stop the battle. It is a flexible framework that can be used in many different ways.

Understanding your differentiator is important. This is a critical component of any company's business strategy. And it is equally important to know how those differentiators translate into your innovation strategy. This helps cascade priorities to every level of the organization. It helps to focus investments on the areas that will create the greatest returns. And it enables you to determine which opportunities will most likely help move the needle for your organization.

Most Companies Invest Too Much in Core

I worked with a major fast-moving consumer goods company. While assisting their IT department, we looked at their investments in technology. They believed they were putting their money into the most valuable projects. But when we analyzed their priorities, we realized that 80 percent of their investments were going into technologies that were core in nature. These didn't help the organization distinguish itself from others.

Marketing and product development were part of their differentiator, as was their unique method of procuring innovations that could be incorporated into their own products. However, although manufacturing, inventory management, and supply chain, for example, were important, they were only core.

Rather than custom-building solutions for core work, they agreed that they would partner, automate, or optimize those processes. Given this, they looked for other software developers that already addressed their core work as part of *their* differentiator.

> How much are you investing on core versus differentiating? Excluding support work, if you are like most organizations, you are spending only about 20 to 30 percent of your money, time, and energy on differentiating investments and 70 to 80 percent on core.

Not surprisingly, they quickly discovered that many of their most complicated projects were in fact technologies that a third party had already developed. Rather than building something new, they realized that buying an existing solution would make more financial sense. Plus, it would allow them to focus on other more important and differentiating work.

As a result, they invested in buying technologies that would suit their needs, maybe with some modifications. In some cases, those solutions didn't meet their needs completely. But they realized that given these capabilities were only core, compromising slightly in the name of expediency and quality was worth the shift. Why should they try to create a one-off solution that would take a ton of money to develop and maintain?

> Move from 80 percent core and 20 percent differentiating to 60 percent core and 40 percent differentiating. By shifting twenty percentage points of your investment from core to differentiating, you double your investments in differentiating without spending any extra money.

When looking at your investments, ask, "Where am I investing my energies?" Most companies intuitively know that you don't want to invest heavily in developing custom solutions for support capabilities. But the waters get muddy when looking at core versus differentiating.

How much are you investing on core versus differentiating? Excluding support work, if you are like most organizations, you are spending only about 20 to 30 percent of your money, time, and energy on differentiating investments and 70 to 80 percent on core. How can you immediately double your impact in the most critical parts of the business? Use different strategies for your core, and then double down on your differentiating investments.

Move from 80 percent core and 20 percent differentiating to 60 percent core and 40 percent differentiating. In other words, shift twenty percentage points of your investments that are currently targeted at core and reinvest them in differentiating capabilities. This will literally double your investments in differentiating without spending any extra money.

AI and the ITM

As of the writing of this book, the allure and potential of artificial intelligence (AI) are stirring considerable excitement and apprehension across the business landscape. Organizations are grappling with AI's dual nature: it represents a remarkable opportunity to redefine operational paradigms, yet it also poses the risk of obsolescence for those slow to adapt, potentially leading to job displacement or competitive disadvantage.

Given the power of AI, its significance to your organization cannot be overstated. However, a critical question to consider is where it fits within the ITM. Should AI become a centerpiece of your organization? Is it a differentiator? For most organizations, it is not. Unless your business specializes in AI as a distinguishing feature, AI is most likely core.

In today's digital economy, integrating AI within your business operations is no longer optional; it's a fundamental requirement. This is the definition of core. It's table stakes. It's the cost of entry. And the stakes will keep increasing over time. It is not about a one-time adoption of AI; it requires continuous enhancement of these capabilities.

AI technologies are instrumental in improving all three levels of activities: support, core, and differentiation. Nevertheless, aspiring to be the leader in AI innovation is misguided for non-AI-centric companies. This pursuit could distract you from focusing on areas where your organization can truly differentiate and deliver unique value.

Given this, for most organizations, the best strategy is to partner with a company that specializes in AI and has it as their differentiator. The key is to make sure AI does not become a bright shiny object for your organization that diverts your attention from what matters most.

SUMMARY: To Be Pivotal, You Must Innovate Where You Differentiate

The ITM will help you focus on what's most important. Print it out, carry it with you everywhere, and then ask yourself the following questions:

- What are we doing that is support? These capabilities create internal value but may not be of interest to your customers. For these, find ways to eliminate, reduce, simplify, or outsource.
- What are we doing that is core? Although customers may not choose to do business with you *because* you excel in these areas, they may leave if you perform poorly. Strive for efficiency by using various optimization or automation techniques, or by partnering with external experts who specialize in these areas.
- What are we doing that is differentiating? Focus the majority of your energy here. Shift investments from core activities to differentiating capabilities.

My clients who have used the ITM to help them reevaluate their investments have generated amazing results as their efforts are now directed toward the most crucial aspects of the business: differentiators that create customer value.

Now that you have the thirty-thousand-foot view on the three levels, let's zoom in on how to find your differentiator.

SECTION THREE

The 5Ds of Differentiation

CHAPTER 5

Today, Tomorrow, and Leverage

If you try to be great at everything, you'll be great at nothing. Being pivotal means focusing your energy on the activities and opportunities that will have the greatest positive impact on your organization. The planted foot. Your differentiator.

Identifying differentiators requires time and guidance. It can be difficult to do on your own because you may be too close, which results in blind spots. However, there is a useful framework that will help you get started: the 5Ds of Differentiation. All good differentiators include each of these five attributes:

1. Distinctive: It sets you apart from the competition.
2. Desirable: People are willing to pay for it, and it creates internal value.

If you try to be great at everything, you'll be great at nothing.

3. Durable: It's difficult for others to replicate.
4. Dynamic: It will remain relevant in a fast-changing world.
5. Disseminated: People inside and outside your organization know, understand, and align with your differentiator.

These Ds are organized into three different categories as seen in the graphic below: today, tomorrow, and leverage.

The 5Ds of Differentiation

TODAY → DISTINCTIVE   DESIRABLE
                ↑   ↑
TOMORROW → DURABLE   DYNAMIC
                       ↓
LEVERAGE → DISSEMINATED

Today

The first two Ds are focused on today's differentiator. How do we compete today? How can we create the greatest amount of value right now? Distinctive and Desirable address the balance of today's needs. Differentiation is what makes you stand out in a crowded market. Why would somebody do business with you and not with someone else? But here's an important point: you may excel at a lot of things, but being good at something doesn't necessarily mean it is what your customers want. You should not do something just because you can do it. Equally, being good at something doesn't necessarily mean it makes you special if everyone else is good at it.

Differentiation is not a product; it is about capabilities. There is always a tendency to talk about a distinctive product. But products have a limited life cycle. We are talking about creating something that stands the test of time—something that you can invest in today and tomorrow, knowing it will continue to be differentiated. Capabilities allow you to go deep, whereas products are more static and need to be reinvented continually.

> **All good differentiators include five attributes:**
> 1. **Distinctive:** It sets you apart from the competition.
> 2. **Desirable:** Customers are willing to pay for it, and it creates internal value.
> 3. **Durable:** It's difficult for others to replicate.
> 4. **Dynamic:** It will remain relevant in a fast-changing world.
> 5. **Disseminated:** People inside and outside your organization know, understand, and align with your differentiator.

Tomorrow

Speaking of limited life cycles, this brings us to the next two Ds: Durable and Dynamic. If your differentiator is product-focused, then you are today-focused only. A product may differentiate now but not necessarily in the future. Companies release new versions of their

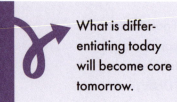
What is differentiating today will become core tomorrow.

phones annually so that they don't fall behind the competition. On the other hand, capabilities give you the ability to do something different in the future without needing to reinvent yourself.

If you don't focus properly, what is differentiating today will become core tomorrow. Competitors copy your products and services. Plus, as the world changes, there are shifts in competition, technology, and buyer behaviors. These will require you to adapt what you offer to meet future needs. Together, these two Ds are about permanence in time, providing the greatest chance that the differentiator will continue to be so tomorrow, not just today. If you are constantly shifting your differentiator, you are constantly pivoting and spinning around in circles—and that's not efficient.

Leverage

Finally, the third category is leverage. This is how you can maximize the value you get from your differentiator. This is about ensuring every employee knows your differentiator and how each individual contributes to it. It is also about communicating your differentiator to the market so that customers and partners know the value you bring. Although this is not specifically about defining your differentiator, it is an extremely powerful way to leverage it.

How the Dimensions Are Interconnected

The 5Ds are designed to help you maximize your investments in the areas that are going to yield the greatest impact. It is about depth and doubling down. It's the planted foot.

The graphic of the 5Ds is drawn in a particular way.

Durable is related to Distinctive. Durable means that what you offer today will remain distinctive in the future. If it's something that someone else can copy or replicate, then it won't continue to be different.

Dynamic links to Desirable. Will what you offer today be desirable tomorrow? Buyer behaviors shift over time, while technologies can disrupt incumbents. You need to adapt to meet future wants and needs of the consumer and buyer.

I realize that remembering the names of all five dimensions can be tricky. Therefore, given the structure, some find it easier to think 2 + 2 + 1: Distinctive today and tomorrow, Desirable today and tomorrow, and Disseminated.

Whatever method you use to remember, this framework will give you clarity about what is most important to your organization.

Go Against What Everyone Else Is Doing

As you will hear repeatedly, differentiators are not products; they are long-lasting capabilities. And a great example of that is DNA Vibe. Although they have a light therapy product called Jazz Band, what makes them special are their unique manufacturing capabilities. They bucked the trend and did exactly the opposite of what the competition had done.

Manufacturing practices have traditionally been organized around centralized, large-scale production involving massive manufacturing plants and warehouses. This approach can hurt the environment as products need to be shipped globally. In addition, it also restricts the available talent pool to a single location and limits the economic benefit to that location.

Given this, cofounder and CEO Perry Kamel set out to create a decentralized and localized manufacturing approach that would reduce the negative impact on the environment and empower communities while increasing resilience in the face of global supply-chain disruptions.

The key was finding a way of doing this so that anyone, regardless of their background or skill set, could participate in creating advanced electronics. The company coined the term "barista proof" to describe this simplified, easily accessible manufacturing process.

To bring this vision to life, DNA Vibe introduced Local Advanced Manufacturing Pods (LAMPs)—small, localized manufacturing centers requiring at most $100,000 in capital investment and occupying no more than four thousand square feet. Strategically placed worldwide, these micro plants would seamlessly blend into urban and rural environments. And they can be up and running in just six months.

Their first LAMP was a three-thousand-square-foot manufacturing center that proved that this decentralized model was viable and highly efficient, with the capacity to produce ten thousand to twenty thousand units of advanced electronic products per month. As the company expanded, additional LAMPs were established, creating a resilient network that could rapidly adapt to changing circumstances and deliver products despite global supply-chain disruptions.

This is an excellent example of all 5Ds in action. They developed a Distinctive capability that no one else has. The ability to launch a new manufacturing facility for under $100,000 with unskilled labor in a matter of months is unheard of. Because of this speed and low cost, it is also quite Desirable. Although they initially produced their own product, they have since expanded to manufacturing products for other electronic companies that can't scale as quickly or inexpensively.

While the concepts behind their LAMPs may appear simple, replicating the process without the necessary knowledge is quite difficult. DNA Vibe established an environment enabling them to swiftly create new LAMPs while maintaining a Durable competitive advantage over those lacking the necessary expertise. And given the nimbleness of this process, it is Dynamic in that they can shift to manufacturing any product in any location, under any circumstances. And lastly, they Disseminated their capability to everyone internally so that the culture was well established.

Mastering and implementing the 5Ds will help you create the greatest impact with the least amount of energy. As a result, you will be—and will remain—pivotal to your customers, employees, partners, and shareholders. You'll be able to firmly plant the stationary foot, providing a solid foundation on which to pivot the moving foot when necessary.

With that as background, let's dive deep into the first D: Distinctive.

Today

CHAPTER 6

Distinctive
What Makes You Special?

Distinctiveness Is Not About You

Once, while running a workshop for a retail firm's executives, I asked about what makes their organization distinctive. They unanimously agreed that it was their cohesive corporate culture, a stark contrast to their competitors' fragmented approaches. This culture, cultivated over decades, undoubtedly set them apart and would be hard for others to replicate. But was it truly distinctive? Maybe not. Distinctiveness is always defined from the customer's point of view, and culture is internal. Very rarely would a customer say, "Oh, I like doing business with you because you have a great culture."

To shift the perspective, I asked the executives, "How does this translate into a tangible benefit for your customers?" Their answer was this: unparalleled, consistent customer service. No matter which employee a customer interacts with, they're guaranteed the same exceptional experience. In a service-centric industry, such consistency is gold. We then delved deeper, strategizing about how to maximize this service-driven culture. The lesson? Distinctiveness lies in the customer's experience, not in internal jargon. It's not about you. It's what you can do for your customers.

> Distinctiveness lies in the customer's experience, not in internal jargon. It's not about you; it's what you can do for your customers.

Bose is a great example of customer focus. Although you might know them as a product company with patented technologies, their dedication to customer service also makes them distinctive. I've heard them say, "If you buy a Bose product, you will be a fan. If your Bose product fails for any reason and you work with our customer service team, you will be a fan for life."

And I can speak from personal experience that that is true. I bought their Sleepbuds. They've been a game changer for helping me sleep in noisy hotels. But after using them for well over a year, I was no longer able to recharge the device. Soon after my product died, Bose released their new version, Sleepbuds II. I contacted them to see if I could get the new model at a discount. Instead, they had me return the old (dead) product, and they shipped me the updated one at no cost. That is service.

Yes, there are other companies with exceptional customer service. But for Bose, incredible technology, combined with outstanding service, makes them unbeatable. This example demonstrates that you can and should have more than one area where you are distinctive. Often it is at the intersection where the real power is found.

How to Find What Makes You Distinctive

How do you find what makes you distinctive?

Too often, companies hold brainstorming sessions with their employees to try to figure it out. But this might not lead you in the right direction. The key is to make sure you have an outside-in approach for identifying your differentiator.

I was working with a hotel chain, and they wanted me to go deep into what makes them distinctive. They planned to assemble a core team of leaders in a room and spend the day discussing their differentiators. I knew this approach would not work and suggested, "We need to bring in an outside point of view."

To guarantee a wide range of perspectives, I ensured that in the room we also had customers and industry experts. In this case, the customers were not guests but rather the owners of the properties that were managed by my client. In addition to customers, we had a couple of consultants who knew the competition and industry trends.

For the first hour and a half, I had the leadership team from the hotel chain share what they thought made them distinctive, different, and valuable. Why do customers do business with them? When they were done, they were convinced they had the right answers.

I then turned to the customers and asked, "How close were they?" Although there were some elements the leadership team got correct, overall they missed the mark. Some of the things that they believed were differentiators turned out to be services that their competitors also provided—and in some instances, their rivals executed those aspects more effectively.

The leaders believed their portfolio diversity and loyalty program benefits were their primary differentiators. However, what customers valued most were the consistent levels of maintenance and management across all geographies. All properties received the same uniform level of service. Had the hotel only looked internally to decide what made them distinctive, they may have invested in less than valuable opportunities. But armed with valid insights from customers, we discussed ways to enhance their capabilities and further leverage them across the organization. They discovered that without an outside perspective, it's difficult to see what truly makes us distinctive or special. External conversations, sometimes with an unbiased external facilitator, are necessary.

> Without an outside perspective, it's difficult to see what truly makes us you distinctive. External conversations, sometimes with an unbiased external facilitator, are necessary.

To complicate matters, if you talk only to your current customers, you might miss big opportunities. What about past customers who no longer do business with you? Why did they leave? What insights can you gather from them? Possibly rethink what you offer to get them back. Or maybe they left for a good reason, and you shouldn't be serving their needs. You can't please everyone—and you shouldn't target everyone.

What about customers you've never done business with? Why not? What do they need? Again, they might not be your ideal target customer. But what if they were?

When seeking feedback, it's common to focus solely on your best customers. However, this strategy can yield lopsided and inaccurate information. To determine what truly makes you distinctive, you must consider the entire spectrum of current, past, and potential customers. The goal is to identify ways to add more value by going deep into what makes you distinctive.

> If you talk only to your current customers, you might miss big opportunities.

To assist you in this process, you can find a list of questions on my website that will help you ask the right customers more effective questions. Get them at:

www.ThePivotalTools.com

Go Broad to Go Deep

To go deep, paradoxically, sometimes you need to think broadly.

I started my business twenty years ago, calling myself a professional speaker. This meant my main income was from getting on stages and delivering presentations. But I'm more than that. I am an innovation expert who delivers content not only through speeches but also through consulting, workshops, educational programs, and mentoring. For me, just being a speaker was too narrow. Sometimes, to go deep, you need to reframe what you do more broadly. How can you take what you do to a deeper level?

> To go deep, paradoxically, sometimes you need to think broadly.

Otis Elevator once believed their distinctiveness lay in elevator manufacturing. However, when they recognized their broader expertise in all aspects of elevators, they ventured into support and service. This move didn't just boost their business—profits from servicing surpassed those from installations—it also allowed them to cater to other brands. Now, services constitute 57 percent of Otis's sales but account for 80 percent of its operating profit. As a result, they've become pivotal to commercial property owners beyond mere installations.

Considering expansion into transportation, people-moving, or mobility sectors might be a logical step for Otis. Such wider viewpoints could reveal opportunities rooted in their unique strengths. However, as they expand, it's crucial they don't dilute their focus. They must build on their foundation rather than shifting to a new one.

Sony also used this broadening strategy to go deep. They were once a leading global electronics manufacturer best known for audio and video equipment. But when they realized they were really in the bigger entertainment business, they identified ways to go deeper with customers, including getting into the content business. Then, they decided to leverage this further, looking beyond home studios and movie theaters. What's the next entertainment horizon for them? Automobiles. Sony has announced that they might be getting into the car business, not because they are automotive experts, but because they are entertainment experts. And as cars move toward autonomous vehicles, you now have a captive audience. At the start of 2023, they announced a partnership with Honda to manufacture the vehicle while Sony leverages their experience with AI, entertainment, virtual reality, and augmented reality. This is a great example of going deeper by expanding their focus. It's not a pivot. They aren't offering something new as a differentiator, but rather they are doubling down on where they already excel. They are just finding new applications.

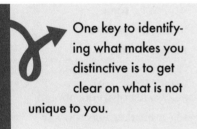

One key to identifying what makes you distinctive is to get clear on what is not unique to you.

Get Clear on What's Not Distinctive

One key to identifying what makes you distinctive is to get clear on what is not unique to you. Getting clarity on who you are not is incredibly helpful in framing where to target your innovation investments. What's not a priority? In other words, identify what's differentiating and what is core. You can answer this from many different perspectives:

- **Which customers are not your target market?** USAA targets only members of the military. Everyone else is not eligible. PURE Insurance offers its services only to a wealthier population. The decisions by these two companies allow them to deliver offerings that are specifically designed for their target market. Which customers won't you serve?
- **Which capabilities and activities will not be a priority for you?** What processes are you willing and able to outsource to a partner? Earlier, we showed that the back-end claims processing system for automotive insurance companies is not a priority, and as a result, most have opted to outsource it to a third party. Gaining clarity on which capabilities aren't distinctive can help you invest where it will make the most difference.
- **What capabilities does the competition already have?** Don't try to replicate or catch up to your competition. If they are already strong in one area, it will be hard to beat them at *their* game. Therefore, choose a different angle and consider some questions: What's a gap in the market? What's an area that no one is addressing that you might be able to handle? Where do your capabilities allow you to create something (or improve something you are already doing) that can help you be distinctive? Progressive insurance serves as a compelling example of this approach.

Although Progressive insurance is now known for Flo and its clever commercials, in the late 1990s, they had a different source of distinction. When Progressive decided to compete against the bigger players, it realized it would struggle to match the more established organizations against their strengths. As a result, they chose to do so by changing the way claims were processed, becoming one of the most profitable firms in the industry. Progressive's loss adjusters operated from vans called Immediate Response Vehicles. These were equipped with cellular communication links and computer workstations long before mobile phones and the internet were a way of life. Driving around their assigned territories, they were often at the scene of an accident before the police. In many cases, claims were processed on the spot, and the company's loss adjusters have been known to hand over a check at the site of an accident.

Progressive recognized areas where they couldn't be distinctive and instead pinpointed a market need that others had overlooked. This alleviated concerns about their being less established than bigger players. They turned a perceived weakness into an advantage by offering something unique, enabling them to compete on their own terms. Such a tactic can be a powerful strategy. I adopt this "turn a weakness into a strength" approach when facing a competitor who is focused on a single industry.

Niche expertise is often seen as an advantage in the innovation space. I, on the other hand, have worked with organizations in nearly every industry. For some customers, my lack of specialization may be perceived as a weakness. I'm often asked, "Why should we hire someone who doesn't know our industry?" I respond with, "This is exactly the reason you need me!"

They look confused, so I continue.

"You already know your industry well. But innovation happens when you connect the dots across industries by bringing the best perspectives of one industry to another. This is how I add value."

From there, I share how some of the biggest breakthroughs have come from people with completely different experiences from the one that the problem suggests. A champagne company helped solve a technical problem regarding bubbles on computer chips. A pizza delivery company provided a solution to an insurance claims tracking problem. Someone in the construction industry solved a complex oil spill issue.

The point is that knowing where to focus and where not to focus is critical to being distinctive.

Dealing with Multiple Customer Types

Quite often you will have multiple types of customers. If so, be sure to have an alignment of what makes you distinctive to your different customers and partners.

Imagine you are running a large chain of hotels with different brands. Each will have its own set of differentiators. Budget hotels will need to be distinctive in ways that business hotels or luxury hotels won't. Business hotels almost always have room service and conference rooms, whereas budget brands may not, and luxury brands might focus on their spas.

> Quite often, you will have multiple types of customers. Therefore, ensure that you have a clear understanding of what makes you distinctive to your various customers and partners.

Equally, you may want to have some unique areas of distinction at a local geographic level. What you offer in New York City or London might not be the same as what you offer in a tourist location like Orlando. A major hotel chain had a high-end whiskey bar in just one location where there was strong demand yet opted for more family-friendly options in children-focused tourist areas.

You might also want to consider that different departments within each property will also have their own unique contributions to the hotel's distinctiveness.

I've found that in general, most organizations have an overall global differentiator—something that applies to every business unit, product line, geography, or department. Then this cascades down to the next level as depicted in the graphic below.

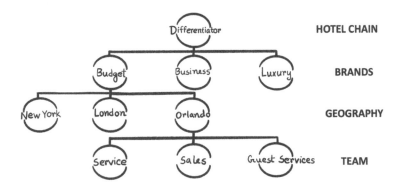

As it turns out, there are multiple dimensions to this concept, making it even more complicated. In the hotel industry, we typically think of the guest as the customer. But consider the fact that in many cases, the hotel chain does not own the property; they only manage it. Therefore, in addition to guests, they have the property owners as customers.

This highlights the fact that most employees and companies have multiple customers.

If you are a parts manufacturer, this would be especially true. Imagine you build and sell seats to the big automotive manufacturers. Although they might be your direct customer, you also need to think about the person who ultimately will buy and drive the car. This might create conflicting demands—and hence conflicting areas of distinction.

Or maybe you work in health care and your customers are patients, doctors, hospital systems, and insurance companies. Each will have different requirements and desires.

To complicate matters further, quite often we also have internal customers. These are the people who need your support. This might be true if you are in an IT role, for instance. Although your customer may be internal, you are creating solutions for external customers too. For example, if you are in a research role that is creating new chemical compounds, you might directly report to an internal group, which ships what you produce externally. Being distinctive is not just about external needs but also internal partners.

In addition, your vendors and suppliers need to be part of the conversation, as they might have unique needs or requirements. All of this can create confusion as you go through this process. The key is to ensure that what makes you distinctive across different customers and partners is cascaded and aligned.

SUMMARY: Be Pivotal by Being Distinctive

You don't get to decide what makes you distinctive—the market does. Therefore, be sure that you think in terms that your customers would use. To be pivotal, you need to offer customers something distinctive that no one else does or can.

It is difficult to determine what makes you distinctive solely by sitting in a conference room with your employees. Given this, get out of your office and listen to and observe what people say and do. Don't just focus on current customers; consider past customers and those you've never done business with. Ask open-ended questions such as the following:

- Why do you choose to do business with us instead of or in addition to our competitors?
- What would make you leave us for another company?
- What do you value most from what we deliver?
- What do we do as well as our competitors (i.e., not a differentiator)?
- What do we do that you don't value? In other words, if we stopped doing it, you would still do business with us.

While going through this process, keep an open mind. Avoid letting your past experiences influence the conversations or your interpretation of what is said. Your blind spots and assumptions can negatively influence the process.

And remember, sometimes to be distinctive, you want to look more broadly so that you can find new ways of going deep. Rethink the business you are in to build stronger, more distinctive relationships with your customers, because being pivotal is about going deep in ways only you can.

Once you know what makes you distinctive, it's time to ensure what you do is wanted by your customers. In other words, your differentiator needs to be desirable.

CHAPTER 7

Desirable

What Do Customers Really Want?

Just Because You Can, Doesn't Mean You Should

After years of development and $2.4 billion in investment, the Revel Casino opened its doors to the Atlantic City Boardwalk on April 2, 2012. This beautiful hotel is top-notch, sophisticated, and classy. I know. I visited it.

But the Revel quickly learned a powerful lesson: being the best doesn't mean you'll be successful. In fact, they failed miserably.

To differentiate itself from other casinos in the area, the Revel did not allow smoking anywhere, and it didn't offer a players' club. They also decided to get rid of the buffet and bus trips to and from the casino. To make it more exclusive, they erected a wall that blocked easy access to the casino from the boardwalk. And to top it off, there was a two-night stay minimum. The goal was to create an exclusive and high-end experience that was different from anything else in Atlantic City.

Unfortunately, the typical person who visits Atlantic City isn't looking for an East Coast version of Las Vegas. The boardwalk attracts families with children who want to sit at the beach, eat cotton candy and hot dogs, and play nickel slots.

Combine their design decisions with a tanked New Jersey economy, increased competition from Pennsylvania casinos, and bad investment decisions, and you have a recipe for disaster.

The Revel Casino opened in April 2012. Two and a half years later it went bankrupt and closed its doors in September 2014. One year after that, the casino was sold for pennies on the dollar at $82 million and remained closed until June 2018, when it opened with a completely different name and concept.

What can we learn from this?

Being Different Is Not the Same as Being Differentiated

The Revel was different and distinctive. It chose policies and a design intended to help it stand out in a crowded market. But these changes were not appreciated by their customers. Serious gamblers wanted to smoke or wanted a players' club. They alienated the more casual gambler by eliminating the buffet and bus trips.

> One of my mantras in business and life is "just because you can, doesn't mean you should."

Innovation is a driver that creates experiences for customers. These need to address both explicit and implicit wants and needs of your market. Clearly, the Revel did not do that. And although one could argue that on some level the casino was attempting to change the overall landscape of gambling in Atlantic City, it failed at that too.

One of my mantras in business and life is "just because you can, doesn't mean you should." Just because they could create a unique experience that rebelled against the design used by every other casino, didn't mean they should.

Ultimately, for any innovation to be successful, it needs to be desirable. This means creating something that your target market will appreciate and be willing to pay for.

> Being desirable means we need to do something that customers want. If nobody wants to buy it, there's no market for what you're doing. Being distinctive yet undesirable to your target market is not differentiation.

The Revel reopened its doors again under new ownership and with a new name: Ocean Resort Casino. With its launch, they "corrected" many of the decisions that were originally made. Smoking is now allowed. The buffet is back. A one-night stay is an option. Stairs were added, making it easy to get to the casino from the boardwalk. They even reconfigured the casino floor to make it less confusing to get from place to place, addressing a common complaint. And the casino is offering more things for kids and families to do, such as a large candy store and "Cereal Town," a restaurant where you can get cereal from around the world all day long.

Time will tell if Ocean Resort Casino will be successful. Although it seems to blend elegance with friendliness—a recipe that has worked for the Borgata (another classier hotel in Atlantic City)—there are still many hurdles to overcome. Regardless of the future of this property, there is a lot to be learned from its past. The rapid and massive failure of the Revel should provide a cautionary tale to any innovator who thinks that being different is the same as being differentiated.

Being desirable means we need to do something that our customer wants to buy. If nobody wants to buy it, there's no market for what you're doing. Being distinctive yet undesirable to your target market is not differentiation. And if you are not desirable, you can never be pivotal. Being of crucial importance to your customer is about being valued.

The Three Levers for Being Desirable

What's desirable is not always obvious. And sometimes we see it more clearly in the rearview mirror. Although some may suggest you want to create solutions for the masses because it increases the volume of potential buyers, that is often not the case. And with electric vehicles, this approach proved to be a recipe for failure.

In 2007, Shai Agassi founded Better Place with the hopes of making electric cars available to the masses. When first launched in Israel, the car had a $30,000 price tag, which was comparable to equivalent gas vehicles. But with a range of only eighty miles, it wasn't very practical or attractive to buyers, resulting in less than 1,500 vehicles being sold. On the other hand, Tesla initially offered a $100,000 status symbol targeted at Silicon Valley millionaires. Although the market was much smaller, the higher price tag allowed them to equip it with a larger battery that lasted nearly 250 miles. Better Place went bankrupt in 2013, while Tesla continues to be one of the most valuable companies in the world by offering lower-cost options today.

How do you create a business that is desirable, without relying on 20/20 hindsight?

I've found that the key to being desirable is to take some advice from Ludwig von Mises, the well-known Austrian economist, who said that three "states" must be present for humans to act and make a shift. Although he looked at it from an economic perspective, I would argue these three states are also the keys to desirability.

1. They must be dissatisfied with their current state (today).
2. They must be able to see a better state (future).
3. They must believe that they can reach the desired state (effort).

Let's deconstruct this. We'll first talk about attracting customers you don't currently have, but the model works perfectly for going deeper with existing customers.

If someone is satisfied with the way things are today (#1), they are unlikely to change. The inertia of the past will keep them where they are. Having said that, there are ways to create dissatisfaction and urgency in the minds of the buyers.

Next, they need to be able to envision a better future (#2). The difference between #1 and #2 is the gap. In theory, the larger the gap, the more likely it is that the buyer will want to make a change and purchase what you are offering. However, this isn't always the case.

#3 is where it becomes interesting. Even if you have an exceptional innovation that fills a gap, the buyer might not be interested if they have low confidence in achieving the desired future state or if they believe the effort required outweighs its value.

> Three states for change:
> 1. They must be dissatisfied with their current state (today).
> 2. They must be able to see a better state (future).
> 3. They must believe that they can reach the desired state (effort).
> —Ludwig von Mises

To be truly desirable, you want your customers to have discomfort with today's situation yet comfort in knowing that the gap can easily be closed.

THE THREE LEVERS OF DESIRABILITY

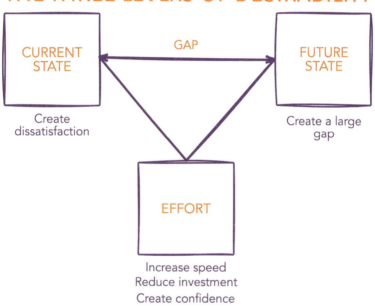

Let's now look at each lever in more detail.

Current State: Create Dissatisfaction

In the mid-1970s, Citibank was the second-largest bank. In 1977, after investing hundreds of millions of dollars in automated teller machine (ATM) technology research and development, Citibank decided to install machines across all of New York City. What should have been a desirable solution was actually very unpopular. The technology was confusing to first-time users, the machines were not always accurate, and they were impersonal. According to one person I spoke with who was involved in the ATM rollout, customers who used ATMs were so frustrated that many closed their Citibank accounts, fearing they might eliminate the human touch of tellers.

The ATM may never have been a hit if it weren't for a natural disaster. February 1978 will always be remembered for a blizzard that dumped as much as four feet of snow in the northeast. In New York City, nearly two feet of snow brought the city to a grinding halt. Banks weren't open. Instead, people got their money by cashing checks at local supermarkets. But most of the supermarkets quickly ran out of money. This created a massive pain for customers.

Where did people turn? The ATMs. It is estimated that during the storms, use of the machines increased by over 20 percent. Soon after, the company introduced its wildly popular slogan: "The Citi Never Sleeps." This was the real birth of the automated teller machine. By 1981, Citibank's market share of New York deposits had doubled, with a lot of the growth attributed to the ATM.

The ATM clearly solved a problem. However, prior to the blizzard, customers were content with obtaining cash from bank tellers and supermarkets, causing the technology to remain stagnant. But when the pain was created by Mother Nature, desirability and demand soon followed.

This story illustrates an innovator's dilemma and opportunity. Brilliant innovations are not necessarily adopted by the masses, and some ideas just need time to incubate and gain acceptance. But will your business survive long enough to see success?

People take massive risks to eliminate their pains but play it safe when it comes to adding convenience. ATMs were primarily about convenience. What did it take for them to become a success? A natural disaster.

In the movie *Field of Dreams*, Ray Kinsella, played by Kevin Costner, hears a voice whispering, "If you build it, he will come." But

> Advertising agencies know that pain sells. Instead of providing peace of mind, insurance companies paint a picture of what would be lost if a catastrophic event occurred and a person was not insured.

with innovation, a more accurate statement is, "If you eliminate a pain, they will come."

We saw the same phenomenon with Zoom when the pandemic hit. A technology that had been around with slow adoption became an overnight must-have.

Of course, a disaster is not always required for the rapid adoption of new technologies. ChatGPT—an AI chatbot—broke all records when it took only five days to reach one million users. Within just two months, over one hundred million users were signed up. The ease of use and the power of the results made it accessible to the masses. Astonishing output from the system (the gap) combined with a user-friendly interface and fast results (effort) proved to be the perfect combination.

Maybe you are fortunate in that what you offer addresses a pain that your customers have. They are already dissatisfied and are hungry for a better solution. But this is not always the case. What if your customers don't know they need you or a new capability you offer? What if your solution is something they truly need, but they don't yet know it? Now we need to turn to plan B: find a way of making them dissatisfied.

Advertising agencies know that pain sells. Instead of providing peace of mind, insurance companies paint a picture of what would be lost if a catastrophic event occurred and a person was not insured. To create that pain, sometimes it takes a bit of creativity. This is something that Boston-based Jordan's Furniture did when it highlighted a concern most of us hadn't considered.

You've probably heard the typical mattress ad that proclaims, "Buy our bed and you will get your best night's sleep ever." If you're tossing and turning, that message hits home. But if you're already cuddled up on a comfy mattress, it might not tempt you. Now, picture Jordan's unique twist: their spokesperson and former co-owner, Eliot Tatelman, eyes twinkling with mischief, vacuums a mattress. He then announces, "If your mattress is ten years old, it weighs twice its original weight due to the dead skin cells and dust mites that accumulate over the years." And for the dramatic finale, he dumps out unsettling gunk from the vacuum. Ew! Suddenly, even if you adore your cozy mattress, if it's got a few years on it, you're thinking of an upgrade.

> Do your solutions address a well-understood pain? Or is what you offer perceived as just a nice-to-have?

Do your solutions address a well-understood pain? Or is what you offered perceived as just a nice-to-have? If the latter, consider creating desirability through discomfort. To move someone, sometimes they need to truly understand the pain of not switching to you.

Future State: Create a Large Gap

OK, you now have something that addresses a pain. Buyers have a high level of dissatisfaction with their current situation and are interested in a better option. But will you offer enough to get them to move?

We now need to consider the gap between their current state and what you create. Imagine you run a bank and want to attract people to put their money into a savings account. The interest rate you offer is 0.001 percent better than your competition. Hmm, is that really going to motivate anyone to shift? Customers might be potentially dissatisfied with what they are currently getting. But unless you have something else of value, they will unlikely be interested in what you have to offer.

And then there's Signet Bank. While other banks were trying to persuade customers to use their credit cards, Signet created a gap so large that everyone wanted in: 0 percent interest on credit card balance transfers. When your bank is charging 15 percent or more, this is a huge gap—and they made it easy to move your accounts. People flocked to give Signet their money. Their credit card business doubled in 1992, in the first year of this offer. It was so successful that in 1994, the credit card division was spun off to create Capital One. Clearly, the bigger the gap, the more appealing the offering.

Effort: Create Confidence in Solution Achievability

One bank I worked with launched a massive education program. They targeted small businesses that have a common concern about taxes and the potential to be audited by the IRS. Their solution was to offer free webinars on the topic. The bank was convinced that their experience in this area was second to none and that companies would switch to them just because of their knowledge. Their expertise made them distinctive, but were the webinars desirable? Not really. Yes, their potential customers were worried (lever #1: dissatisfaction with the current state), they wanted the reduced risk of being audited (lever #2: the desired future state), and the webinars had no cost (one aspect of lever #3). The problem was that these companies had a low level of confidence (another aspect of lever #3) that watching a webinar was going to make their employees smart enough to get the work done. There is a difference between being told how to do something and having the skills to implement the suggested solutions. When the bank started to offer customized services where they would review a customer's financial situation and help them take the steps necessary to reduce the risk of an audit, customers came flocking.

This final lever is the one that is most often missed or ignored. Offering something much better than what's out there doesn't necessarily mean that people will want to do business with you. Why? Because they must believe that it is easy enough for them to get the benefits you offer.

If you work for a major corporation that has invested millions (and millions) in installing SAP company-wide, no matter how great a new piece of enterprise software is, it is unlikely you will make the switch as the effort is too difficult.

Being desirable is more than just wanting what you offer. Being desirable also means that what you offer must seem attainable. You need to make sure the buyer believes they can achieve the future state with your solution with minimal time and effort and with a high level of confidence.

> There are three aspects of the effort lever:
> - Time to value (speed)—How long will it take for the results to be produced?
> - Cost and effort (investment)—How much money and resources are required?
> - Certainty of outcome (confidence)—How likely will the results be achieved? How confident are we that the gap can be closed?

There are three typical "aspects" of embracing a shift that you want to consider for lever #3:

- Time to value (speed)—How long will it take for the results to be produced?
- Cost and effort (investment)—How much money and resources are required?
- Certainty of outcome (confidence)—How likely is it that the results will be achieved? How confident are we that the gap can be closed?

Before the pandemic, I traveled about 150 to 200 nights a year. To maintain my status, I tried to limit my travel to one or two airlines. There was one airline that I almost never flew because their routes were less convenient in most cases. When I was offered gold status for a year, I figured I would give them a try. I was happy enough with the other airlines (lever #1) and didn't really see the better future (lever #2). But giving me the free status upgrade for the year addressed lever #3. It made that airline more desirable—at least for a while. In the end, because I never saw the gap improve (the routes were still less convenient and the planes were no better), I went back to my original carriers. This shows why all three levers are so critical. Addressing just one of them will be a recipe for long-term failure.

Let's consider the "confidence" aspect. This is the one that trips people up a lot. Just because you can make it easy from a time and cost perspective doesn't make it desirable. How confident are your customers that you can deliver? Confidence can come from simplicity. How hard will it be for your customer to do the necessary work? You want the right balance of making it simple and accessible, yet you want to make sure the customers are confident they have enough detail to get it right.

A colleague of mine did some tests selling an information product. One offer was fifteen one-hour videos on how to create a better website that sells. The other offer was three one-hour videos plus twelve bonus videos. The bonuses were designed to be truly optional and only for those who wanted to go even deeper. The only change was the marketing copy; the prices were identical. The second offer was by far the bigger seller. The buyer had a higher level of comfort with their ability to watch the three required videos, and they liked the bonus videos for when they got stuck. This increased the "speed" and "confidence" aspects.

How confident are your customers that your solution will get them the desired result?

There are two other aspects of this lever to consider:

1. If competitors are well established and switching isn't easy, potential customers won't be enticed to change. Overcoming this barrier is crucial. I had a customer relationship management (CRM) system and a separate autoresponder for newsletters, with over ten thousand customers and complex integrations. Switching seemed daunting until I discovered SpeakerFlow, a Zoho-based toolset for speakers, trainers, and consultants. They transferred my data, recreated logic flows, and integrated with my websites, making the switch seamless. I wouldn't have been able to switch systems without their help because it would have been too complicated for me to do on my own.
2. If your offering is easily replaceable, you'll stay desirable only until competitors catch up. Instead of locking people in, which may alienate customers, develop remarkable solutions that make them unwilling to switch, even if it's effortless. Aim to be the top choice now and in the future. When you are irreplaceable, you are pivotal.

Shifting the Gap to Be More Desirable

Although we intuitively believe that a large gap drives people to shift, in many cases, a smaller gap might make something more desirable. When the gap is too large, the results seem unattainable.

> Although we intuitively believe that a large gap drives people to shift, in many cases, a smaller gap might make something more desirable. When the gap is too large, the results can seem unattainable.

A good way to visualize this is to imagine you're an average American household with $38,000 in debt, not including your mortgage. You are struggling to pay your bills. If you were in this situation, which magazine article would be more appealing to you: "Get Out of Debt Fast" or "Become a Millionaire Next Year"?

Although the second headline, "Become a Millionaire Next Year," creates a bigger gap between your current and future state, it might seem too ambitious and too difficult to achieve the desired result. Only after you are out of debt would financial wealth seem like a possibility. You must "meet people where they are." That is, you need to solve their pain (e.g., debt) before you can get them excited about any other gain (e.g., riches).

We see this in a wide variety of other areas.

Often, people prefer to stick with familiar technology instead of learning new ones, even if the updated tools are more advanced with better features. Or, unless someone is extremely uncomfortable with their current job situation, they may prefer to stay with their current employer instead of seeking a new one. We often go for what is easy rather than what we really want, especially if the effort is perceived as too large.

Gaps aren't always obvious, and they can grow or shrink by shifting perspective. In 2008, we experienced a major recession along with four-dollars-per-gallon gasoline. Money was tight, and people were picky about where to spend their hard-earned cash. During a time of economic difficulty and soaring fuel prices, which car was most popular? A hybrid? A fuel-efficient car with over thirty miles-per-gallon

(MPG)? An ultra-inexpensive car? A reliable import? Interestingly, the two most popular vehicles were the Ford F150 (16 MPG) and Chevy Silverado (17 MPG) pickup trucks, with combined sales of nearly one million vehicles. Why? According to Jeff Bartlett, deputy online editor of autos for *Consumer Reports*, when times are tough, "buyers shift from what they want to what they need." He continued to say that "pickups are a solution to a need" because they can be used for towing, off-roading, and cargo-hauling.

> **Often, people prefer to stick with familiar technology instead of learning new ones, even if the updated tools are more advanced and have better features. We tend to choose what is easy rather than what we really want, especially if the effort required is perceived as too great.**

Despite concerns about the economy and high gas prices, consumers in 2008 were focused on the versatility of vehicles that could serve purposes beyond transportation. The pickup trucks cost more money and had worse fuel efficiency than passenger cars. But by highlighting the multifunctional features of the vehicle, the mindset of buyers was shifted, and greater desirability was created.

How I Used the Three Levers in My Business

In this section on desirability, we talked extensively about getting someone to switch to you or get them to stay and not look elsewhere. The same logic applies to going deeper with existing customers.

Each chance to go deeper requires that your customers believe that what you are offering will solve a large enough problem, with a high level of confidence that it can be done quickly, inexpensively, and with low risk.

In my work, I constantly look at this model of desirability—particularly the "confidence" aspect. If a company sees value in developing a culture of innovation, yet they don't have the ability to do it effectively, this creates both dissatisfaction (#1) and a gap (#2). To be an attractive partner for a company, I must reduce the client's effort and investment while assuring them of achieving the desired results (#3).

One question I asked myself while designing one of my programs was, "How can I make it less expensive without impacting the quality of the results?" The answer was a series of weekly prerecorded videos that are released to everyone before our live calls. This allows for real-time interactions to be high-value and customized rather than rote presentations and storytelling. Less time with me on the calls means lower costs to the client.

Equally important, I needed to find a way to reduce the amount of time participants spent each week doing the work required of them by the program. To achieve this, the videos were condensed to include only the most crucial content, with bonus materials provided for those willing to invest extra time. The program's agenda is always custom designed to laser focus on the most significant pain points.

Also, to make sure the clients are getting the greatest impact, the work is centered on solving real-world problems and finding high-value opportunities. Participants learn new skills while creating real value by doing work they would be doing anyway.

By keeping the three levers in mind while going deeper, you will find that your differentiator and the associated offerings are truly desirable. Customers will achieve the following:

- Get something they want and need
- See the brighter future that will call them forward

- Have the confidence that you can get them there with the lowest investment in terms of time, money, or resources while mitigating risk and complexity

As an aside, if your customers don't find your offering desirable, it might not be because they don't want it. It might be simply because of the way you communicated it. The third pillar—confidence in being able to get results quickly with little effort—might be the issue. Quite often what makes something desirable is confidence in results being achieved. And you need to make sure your customers understand the power and simplicity of working with you. This is all a winning combination.

The only way to be pivotal is to be truly desired by your customers. Although your differentiator must be externally desirable, it must also be internally desirable.

• • •

Internal Desirability: It's Not Just What the Customers Want

Beyond customers, desirability also means that it must be good for you and your organization. After all, offering something everyone loves while going bankrupt in the process is certainly not desirable. Focusing on only external needs when the needs of your employees are ignored is a recipe for disaster. We saw this with the Homejoy story.

Here are a few questions to get you thinking about the internal desirability of your differentiator.

- **Will your differentiator be profitable, or will you end up losing money?** Unless you work for a nonprofit, you need to make money. And even if you work for a non-profit, you need to be fiscally responsible. A loss-leader approach is not a long-term strategy. In November 2022, Walt Disney's chief executive Robert Iger told employees that he would chase profitability over growing subscriber numbers at Disney's streaming services. Losing money while adding subscribers is not sustainable.

- **Will your differentiator enhance what you already do, or will it be a distraction?** The last thing you want to do is add confusion to an already burned-out organization. Clarity is critical. Alignment with what you have done, what you are doing, and what you should be doing is critical. A classic example of this is when McDonald's launched their Arch Deluxe in 1996, a burger aimed at adult consumers. Not only was this a huge commercial flop, as their core customers rejected the idea, but employees were frustrated because the burger was complicated to make and required new sauces, buns, and fresh lettuce. This is an example of a company going deeper with the wrong audience.

> Desirability must also be good for you and your organization. Focusing on only external needs when the needs of your employees are ignored is a recipe for disaster.

- **Will your differentiator make you more attractive to your employees, or will it leave you searching for talent?** Attracting and retaining your best people is critical. Losing institutional knowledge will drain your company. Spending all your time trying to bring in new people will distract you. If your differentiator is too far from where you are today, you might induce burnout. Get it right from the beginning, and then go deeper. Shifting your differentiator away from what made you attractive in the first place can cause an employee exodus. A garment manufacturer took pride in offering exclusively U.S.-made products, asserting that they delivered superior quality and provided better working conditions for employees. However, in an attempt to expand the business, the company chose to adjust its strategy. Instead of focusing on premium, high-quality clothing, they shifted toward more affordable products produced abroad. Although this attracted cost-conscious buyers, their target market stopped purchasing their clothing. In addition, this move created resentment among employees who felt deceived and no longer wanted to be part of the company's budget mindset.

- **Will your differentiator build a long-term relationship with your customers, or are you merely creating transactions?** If you don't go deep with your customers, you might spend all your time trying to recruit new ones. This puts an incredible strain on your organization. Sales teams need to work overtime. Customer support organizations need to do a lot of handholding for newer customers. Even your product development teams will be stretched, as they must keep learning about the needs of new customers rather than having that deep knowledge of what is truly needed for repeat customers. A software firm I'm familiar with quickly expanded its customer base but faced high churn rates. Many clients felt the product didn't solve big enough problems, leading them to seek better solutions. This churn strained the sales team, causing some to leave. Plus, the software's tricky setup led to customer support attrition. To counter this, the company shifted focus to fewer, high-value clients, which improved both client and employee retention.

Be sure to ask the questions above whenever you consider any change initiative. Not focusing on internal desirability might leave your planted foot unhinged. You may lose money, lose employees, and even lose more customers.

SUMMARY: Desirability Drives Being Pivotal

Being pivotal means you are "of crucial importance." And to achieve this level of importance, you must be desirable.

Achieving the right balance between meeting customer needs and your own internal needs is critical for long-term, sustainable competitive advantage. If you get this wrong, you might have to pivot repeatedly. The planted foot must provide a level of stability and desirability.

To help you move in the right direction, remember that your differentiator needs to address the three levers of change in your market:

1. *Today*—There must be dissatisfaction with the current state.
2. *Future*—There must be a large enough gap between today and the possible future.
3. *Effort*—You must ensure that the path toward success is fast, inexpensive, and reliable.

The "effort" lever is critical and often overlooked. For people to embrace a shift, you need to ensure that you address three aspects:

- Time to value—speed
- Cost and effort—investment
- Certainty of outcome—confidence

In addition to making sure your differentiator is desirable externally, you also want to ensure it is desirable internally so that it is profitable, not a distraction, and attractive to your employees.

- Will your differentiator be profitable, or will you lose money?
- Will your differentiator enhance what you already do, or will it be a distraction?
- Will your differentiators make you more attractive to your employees, or will it leave you searching for talent?
- Will your differentiators build a long-term relationship with your customers, or are you merely creating transactions that lead to internal burnout?

When you have a differentiator that is both internally and externally desirable, you are on the path toward being pivotal.

When your differentiator is both distinctive and desirable, you have a powerful differentiator today. But will it stand the test of time? In exploring the next D, Durable, we learn how to stay distinctive in the future.

TOMORROW

CHAPTER 8

Durable

How Can You Be Difficult to Duplicate?

Don't Do the Hard Work for Your Competition

I worked with a home assurance company that fixes appliances when they break. Customers pay a flat monthly subscription, giving them peace of mind that if something malfunctions, they can get it fixed for a small service fee.

When I asked the top leaders of this business, "What is your differentiator?," everybody agreed it was their pricing models. They believed they were unique and sophisticated. They put a lot of money into analyzing historical statistics of repair costs to determine a subscription fee that was reasonable to the customer yet profitable for the business. Time, money, and resources were spent building these skills and developing these models.

When I asked how soon the competition replicated any new pricing model after they were introduced, I was told that it happened, on average, within two weeks. Two weeks!

> In today's environment, organizations often turn to technology as their differentiator. But the human element is much more durable.

This is not a unique differentiator. It is certainly not durable. This was the company doing the hard work for their competition. The competition watched what they did and followed suit. This would lead to more spinning, always trying to stay one step ahead of their competition.

After further exploration, we determined that the company's true differentiator was its extensive network of repair people. They had technicians with a wide range of experiences. Their network had great geographical coverage, and the skill levels were best in class.

This massive network would be extremely difficult for a competitor to recreate. As a result of this insight, they reallocated their investments to nurture their network of technicians, providing them with free training and assisting them in growing their businesses, even if it meant working with a competitor (they did not require exclusive arrangements). The members of their repair network were then dedicated to the company, and it created the best level of service for their customers.

Your differentiator needs to be durable. Although one definition of durable is "able to resist wear," it also implies enduring or long-lasting. It is the latter definition that I use here. Durable means that your distinctiveness stands the test of time by being non-copyable and non-duplicable.

You need to somehow protect your competitive position. Although it might be distinctive today, will it remain so tomorrow? You can, of course, protect your position in the market with legal structures such as patents and trademarks. But more often, the key is to focus on differentiators that will be difficult for others to replicate. There's no sense in creating a capability, offering, product, or service that others can easily copy. You want a solidly planted foot that will stay there.

Although Coca-Cola is known for its soft drinks and other beverages, what is most durable about them is their brand recognition. They've leveraged this brand beyond beverages by creating lines of clothing with their distinctive red color and lettering. Replicating this would be very difficult for the competition.

> Your differentiator is much more than something unique that people want. Having only those two dimensions is like having a table with only two legs—not very stable.

As we saw with the home assurance example above, sometimes what you think is your differentiator might be a detractor. It could be taking your eye off something more important.

In today's environment, organizations often turn to technology as their differentiator. But the human element is much more durable. Unless you are in a technology business (and even when you are), it is way too easy for someone else to recreate your technology—especially if it is software. There are talented coders around the world ready to take your idea and make it even better.

A client of mine invested heavily in a reservation system that was second to none. They were the first to offer this to their customers. During a brainstorming session, nearly everyone in the room (all senior executives) felt this was their differentiator. They were first and hence distinctive. They knew their customers wanted it as it made their lives better. But they didn't consider the durability dimension. I pointed out that what they created was great but would soon be copied. In fact, once their system was released to the public, their competitors went

> If someone can replicate what you do, you've done the homework for the competition. It's not a differentiator. For this reason, durability is the result of something other than a product or technology.

to work replicating and improving the system. I can honestly say that what their biggest competitor offers is better for a number of reasons. Interestingly, my client never went back to try to improve their system to be on par with (or better than) their competition. As a result, they now have an inferior product that is far from a differentiator.

Your differentiator is much more than something unique that people want. Having only those two dimensions is like having a table with only two legs—not very stable.

With companies that are product or technology focused, it's often easy enough for someone to reverse engineer what they've done. Why? Some companies are fast followers. Their entire business strategy is not to be first to market but to be skilled at quickly reverse engineering what someone else has done. If someone can replicate what you do, you've done the homework for the competition. It's not a differentiator. For this reason, durability is the result of something other than a product or technology.

Durability Is Beyond Products and Technology

In the world of sanitary products and systems, one company stands out for its longevity and success: Geberit. This Swiss multinational group started as a plumbing company way back in 1874 and has since expanded globally to operate in most European countries and several other continents. They have mastered the design, production, and installation of sanitary products and systems, including pipes, fittings, valves, toilets, bidets, urinals, showers, and bathtubs.

Their success has been attributed to the company's commitment to innovation and sustainability, which has resulted in over one thousand patents, water-saving technologies, recycled materials, and renewable energy sources. But patents aren't the only way Geberit has created a durable company.

> What makes many companies durable is some sort of network. Not a computer network but a collaboration of people, products, or organizations.

They also focus on building long-term relationships with customers, suppliers, and installers, rather than treating each project as a one-off. In addition, they look at the end-to-end process of manufacturing, distribution, and installation. Their strategy involves working closely with plumbers, wholesalers, and end users to create demand for their products and services.

Geberit's success can also be attributed to its strong brand reputation and loyal customer base. With a market share of around 40 percent in Europe and net sales of CHF 3.4 billion (approximately $3.7 billion) in 2022, Geberit is truly an outlier in its industry, with multiple facets of differentiation that make it difficult to duplicate.

When I look at some of the most successful companies, what makes them durable is some sort of network. Not a computer network but a collaboration of people, products, or organizations. Geberit did this through its network of plumbers and wholesalers.

Focus on Integration

We see this network effect in technology companies like Apple. Part of their success can be attributed to their ecosystems which serve

> Being durable sometimes means integrating in a way that makes it difficult for the competition to break in.

as durable differentiators. When Apple introduced the iPod, it wasn't the first mp3 player, but it was the first to link hardware with the ability to buy individual songs. The real innovation at that time was iTunes, a network of artists and record labels. This integration made other mp3 players less appealing and made it more difficult to switch away from the iPod. And the interoperability of Apple products also serves as a differentiator. With iCloud, hardware works seamlessly together, allowing devices to connect automatically and enabling a user to control multiple devices with ease. This level of integration makes switching to an Android phone nonsensical for those invested in Apple's ecosystem. Yes, they have great technology with a great design. However, in these fast-changing times, hardware and software are often only core, especially in a space where new products are launched every year.

Being durable sometimes means integrating in a way that makes it so the competition can't break in. If you can set up an ecosystem that your customers join, it makes them less likely to leave. If your home automation is through Google's Nest, any devices you add in the future will almost certainly be compatible with Nest. It would be hard for a Google Nest home to switch to Amazon Smart Home products. It's easier having one system than maintaining multiple hubs, accounts, and automation routines.

Insurance companies work hard to "bundle" policies, like home, auto, and business, because customers with multiple policies stay longer. Bigger firms also offer specialty insurance, like for boats or motorcycles. Having a single contact for all insurance makes it harder for customers to leave. When you're deeply integrated into customers' lives, you become pivotal.

Another way to be pivotal and distinctive in the long run is to build desirable and durable capabilities that create customer value. A great example of this is the second-largest privately held company in the United States, Koch Industries.

> To be distinctive in the long run, build desirable and durable capabilities that create customer value.

Capability as a Durable Differentiator

Koch Industries, with revenues exceeding $125 billion, owes much of its success to its unique Principle Based Management™ (PBM) philosophy that emphasizes decentralization and employee empowerment.

Koch Industries is involved in hazardous businesses like asphalt, paper, pulp, oil, and gas. Using their employee empowerment philosophy, Koch Industries made safety the responsibility of every employee instead of relying solely on a few safety engineers to identify unsafe conditions. Employees were rewarded for both uncovering unsafe conditions and discovering safer ways to conduct business. This initiative resulted in 35 to 50 percent improvements each year in the number and severity of accidents across the company.

I witnessed the power of Koch Industries' PBM approach when they acquired Georgia-Pacific, a manufacturer of commodity paper-based products like Dixie Cups and Brawny paper towels. Back in 2005, Georgia-Pacific was struggling. Upon acquiring the company, Koch Industries swiftly implemented its PBM philosophy, revolutionizing the entire organization.

A notable change was in their reward system. While Georgia-Pacific traditionally incentivized employees to meet budgets and quarterly projections, Koch Industries took a different approach. They motivated their workforce based on contributions to long-term value creation, aligning rewards with meaningful outcomes instead of simply meeting targets. This shift in focus led to Georgia-Pacific's remarkable turnaround, ultimately allowing the company to thrive.

Koch Industries has been using PBM for over five decades. It is built into the company's DNA. It would be nearly impossible for another company to copy what they've done. This makes it extremely durable.

Customers may not explicitly identify Koch's PBM as a differentiator, yet it offers numerous benefits. The approach fosters efficiency, cost-effective products, and customer-driven innovation. Additionally, it allows for swift adaptation to market changes and customer preferences. Koch Industries' PBM has been a key factor in its sustained growth and value creation for customers. Koch has its planted foot solidly grounded with its PBM. It drives decision-making and results in a differentiator that can't be replicated.

Although your organization might not be able to replicate what Koch Industries has achieved, ask yourself, "What capabilities do I have that I can leverage to create a durable source of competitive advantage?" This should help you clarify which investment decisions will stand the test of time.

SUMMARY: Being Durable Leads to Being Pivotal

When your differentiator is durable, you become pivotal to your customers. No one can offer what you do the way you do. If you want to be pivotal, ensure you don't do the hard work for your competition. Create something that will be difficult for competitors to replicate.

The following are some ways to remain durable, and hence distinctive, in the future:

- Focus on developing hard-to-imitate capabilities rather than on products, services, or technologies that can be reverse-engineered and copied.
- Build sustainable networks of individuals and organizations that yield value and present obstacles for duplication.
- Establish a well-known and respected brand.
- Create a complex infrastructure that would be difficult for others to build.
- Integrate your offerings so that once someone is in your ecosystem, they will struggle to switch to a competitor.
- Create a culture of differentiation that generates value for customers. This is often difficult to replicate.

These elements may take a long time to establish, but once you do, they will help you withstand the test of time.

We now have three anchors for the planted foot: distinctive, desirable, and durable. With that level of stability, you are now ready to pivot from a place of power when needed. We now turn to long-term desirability and the fourth D: Dynamic.

CHAPTER 9

Dynamic

How Can You Stay Desirable?

So far, we've explored when and where to "go all in." However, there are times when it's crucial to recognize when to fold (borrowing another poker term) or, in business terms, when to pivot. In essence, we must change direction to remain desirable in the future. As the world evolves, so must we. We need to be dynamic, adapting in ways that keep us desirable both today and in the future.

> As the world evolves, so must we. We need to be dynamic, adapting in ways that keep us desirable both today and in the future.

A well-documented example is Tiny Speck, a San Francisco–based company that wanted to revolutionize the gaming industry. They had high hopes. Their first game, Glitch, launched on September 27, 2011, to much fanfare. But despite their best efforts, they didn't get enough

> Ideally, you first want to have a firmly planted foot before pivoting so that when you change direction, it is built on top of a stable source of differentiation.

players to make it profitable, and the company was forced to shut it down a year later.

Although many might throw in the towel at that point, the development team noticed that the chat functionality within the game had become a hit with players and employees alike. The game's differentiator eventually launched a new product.

A year later, Slack was born. This chat-based collaboration tool changed the way teams communicate and work together. It was so successful that in 2019 they went public, and in 2021 Salesforce, one of the world's largest software companies, acquired Slack for a whopping $27.7 billion.

By taking a chance on a seemingly insignificant aspect of a failed product, they created something pivotal: a tool that empowers teams to collaborate and communicate. I bring up the story of Tiny Speck here for two reasons. First, they were never desirable enough to drive profitability and therefore never really had a solid differentiator. Second, when they realized they wouldn't attract enough customers, they dynamically pivoted in a way that made them desirable. In this situation, as is often the case, being dynamic involves looking beyond the product and focusing on capabilities. This is an example of a failure leading to the pivot. But that's not the most effective way to be dynamic. Ideally, you first want to have a firmly planted foot before pivoting so that when you change direction, it is built on top of a stable source of differentiation.

Snowdevil successfully transitioned from focusing on products to emphasizing capabilities, building on their existing strengths. Founded in 2004, they initially sold snowboarding gear. Dissatisfied with e-commerce options, a founder crafted his own solution. Quickly, they realized their e-commerce platform outshined their products. By 2006, they shifted from selling gear to promoting their platform, Shopify. Transitioning from a product to capability focus, they became a powerhouse, generating over $5 billion in annual revenues.

To be dynamic, you must know when to shift to remain desirable—both externally and internally. Earlier, we talked about Progressive's Immediate Response Vehicles. This was their attempt to create a distinctive and desirable offering to compete against the bigger players. However, over time, the company abandoned this strategy. Why? It was no longer internally desirable. It was holding the company back from scaling the business. If you need to invest in a huge van network to monitor accidents, that's not efficient. In addition, it was no longer externally desirable. As new technology emerged, they could do everything digitally rather than physically. This dynamic shift helped position Progressive as a market leader today, leveraging what they did so well in the past.

Being pivotal means that *sometimes* you need to pivot.

Stay Desirable

The first three Ds form the basis of a long-lasting differentiator. For most organizations, these are the three to focus on initially. Get these right and you should be in good shape—at least for a while. However, there is one other aspect that needs to be considered: future desirability.

What would make you less desirable tomorrow? What types of external shifts would have your customers looking elsewhere to meet their needs?

It might be a new competitor with a significantly more desirable, completely different offering. It could be an emerging technology that makes what you offer less desirable. Or it might be some societal shift that moves your business toward becoming irrelevant.

Until now, we have discussed how and when to plant your foot and go deep. Utilize the first three Ds to build a solid base. Once that is accomplished, you are prepared to address future changes. After going deep and constructing your platform, it's time to identify situations that may require a pivot.

To stand the test of time, you need to make sure your differentiator is Dynamic. This means that your current offerings must remain desirable in the future. To clarify, when I use the word dynamic, I am not implying the dictionary definition of "constant change"; rather, I suggest being adaptable enough to change when circumstance dictates. To be pivotal, you must know when and how to pivot from a place of power. The goal of being dynamic is for you to remain desirable in the future.

Assuming you have your stationary foot solidly planted, how do you know where and when to pivot? What might trigger your need to be dynamic? A good starting point is to examine the impact of new and disruptive technologies.

Disruptive Technologies

Imagine you are an executive at UPS. What market shifts would keep you up at night?

Maybe it's the fact that Amazon announced they are getting into the logistics business to compete head-to-head with UPS and FedEx. Maybe it is the rapid development of drone technologies or autonomous vehicles to deliver packages.

But there is something that has the potential to completely disrupt UPS and the entire supply chain: 3D printing. This is something that shipping companies need to consider if they want to remain pivotal.

In today's world, materials, parts, and finished products are shipped all over the globe. Raw materials are shipped to parts manufacturers who ship their items to a company that assembles them into a finished product. The finished product is then shipped to a warehouse that ships it to the end customer. That's a lot of shipping.

But consider how 3D printing has the potential to shake things up. Instead of shipping products, you simply email a blueprint, and you "print" the finished product where it is to be used, when you want it. The logistics network is pretty much eliminated. Imagine a world where 3D printers are as widely available as inkjet printers.

Knowing that 3D printing could be a major disruption to their business, UPS has launched an "on-demand 3D printing manufacturing network" to stay ahead of the game. Additionally, they have introduced 3D printing capabilities in many of their stores. However, this shift does not leverage UPS's past differentiators. Will it become a new differentiator, or will it be a distraction? Only time will tell if this change in direction will pay dividends. Nevertheless, their thought process of exploring ways to stay relevant in the future is admirable. The technology is indeed evolving at a rapid pace.

In 2016, a division of Airbus released the world's first 3D-printed electric motorcycle. Soon after, BMW announced its plans to create motorcycle frames using 3D printing. 3D printing is even being used to build large structures such as bridges, houses, and rocket fuselages.

3D printing is not just for "hard" items like motorcycles. In Europe, they are 3D printing steaks using lab-grown meat, resulting in a product that can be customized to your desired level of marbling and fat content. Although it might be a while before this is mainstream, I wouldn't be

> Being dynamic does not mean major technological changes. Being dynamic is about responding to external changes so that you can remain desirable in the future.

surprised if this shows up in high-end restaurants in the near future. Of course, it is easy to get seduced by the coolness of technology. But don't be distracted by it unless it truly aligns with your differentiator or you are concerned it has the potential to disrupt your industry. This is the key to making sure your business is Dynamic.

Being dynamic does not mean major technological changes. Being dynamic is about responding to external changes so that you can remain desirable in the future. Will 3D printing result in UPS not being needed for their delivery services? Probably not. But it is smart to augment their brown trucks and planes with these technologies—as long as it does not become a distraction. Will 3D-printed steaks kill the cattle industry? Unlikely. But it will have an impact. Instead of fighting disruptive technologies, how can you embrace them? Leverage your differentiators to help you get a foothold before you become irrelevant.

It Goes Beyond Technology

The need to be dynamic doesn't only arise from disruptive technologies. It could also stem from competitors drawing away your customers because what they offer is simply more desirable than what you provide.

We used to be fine with deliveries taking a week or more. But now, with Amazon Prime, you are pretty much guaranteed two-day delivery with free shipping. And now you can get some items in an hour. This "more desirable" offering is disruptive, setting a high benchmark for other delivery businesses by establishing elevated customer expectations.

"More desirable" can take many forms. Who would have thought a reptile could cause heartburn for the largest insurance company? As we explored earlier, State Farm has a durable differentiator with its agent network and its "Like a good neighbor, State Farm is there" jingle. However, because of greater transparency on rates across providers, customers now see lower-cost options. Geico's "Fifteen minutes can save you 15 percent or more" ad campaign with their British gecko has forced the market leader to also take a stand on cost. Many State Farm television commercials now say, "When you want the real deal, like a good neighbor, State Farm is there." We all want a good deal. And if we can get the best agent network with it, that's a powerful one-two combination. Being durable doesn't mean anything if you can't remain desirable.

> The need to be dynamic doesn't only arise from disruptive technologies. It could also stem from competitors drawing away your customers because what they offer is simply more desirable than what you provide.

This highlights an important point. You can either offer your products and services for less money (which means you are a commodity), or you can offer something no one else can that customers truly value. But we live in a dynamic world, and what customers value changes over time. What was important yesterday may not be important tomorrow.

Sometimes the need to be dynamic has nothing to do with technology or the competition. It can be through societal or cultural shifts. Over the past few years, "sustainability" through lower carbon emissions has impacted many industries, driving the need to

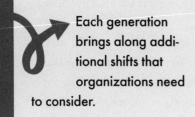

Each generation brings along additional shifts that organizations need to consider.

dynamically change product design. Electric cars, for example, have become cool, negatively impacting sales of gas-engine vehicles. Buying "green" is trendy, moving people toward more environmentally friendly options. And food manufacturers have seen the value of shifting toward healthier alternatives through the elimination of trans fats, added sugars, and artificial ingredients.

But what do you do when your entire business is based on something harmful? This was the dilemma faced by Philip Morris International (PMI), the manufacturer of Marlboro and other cigarette brands. They chose to make a dramatic and dynamic shift. Instead of asking, "How can we sell more cigarettes when health concerns are reducing consumption?," they took a counterintuitive approach. Instead, they decided to answer the question, "How can we exit the cigarette business altogether?" According to their website, "At PMI, it is our ambition to replace cigarettes with science-based, smoke-free products as soon as possible. These products provide nicotine without burning, making them a much better alternative to cigarettes." Considering that cigarettes accounted for nearly all of their revenue, this was a monumental shift. To pursue this direction, they invested $4.5 billion in developing iQOS, a device that heats tobacco rather than burning it, which significantly reduces the release of toxins. It has been available in some countries since 2014. How well has this worked for them? According to published reports, smoke-free products accounted for approximately 35 percent of their revenues in the first quarter of 2023. Although the transition from selling cigarettes to selling devices that heat tobacco represents a significant shift, it has both proven to be a financial win for PMI and offered a potential health improvement for smokers seeking a cigarette-like experience.

And each generation brings along additional shifts that organizations need to consider. Millennials and Gen Zers are shifting consumer behavior as they are more likely to invest in socially responsible and ethical companies, as well as new technologies such as cryptocurrencies. They often prioritize experiences over material possessions and are more likely to spend money on travel, dining out, and entertainment. A smaller proportion of these younger generations are becoming homeowners as they face challenges such as student debt, stagnant wages, and rising housing costs. And they value job flexibility, work-life balance, and purpose over traditional job security, leading to a rise in freelance, gig-based, and remote work. Each of these can impact your organization in a number of ways.

> Your need to be dynamic might not necessarily be driven by a nimble company, a new app, or some whiz-bang technology. It could be the result of economic and societal shifts that impact the buying decisions of your customers. What was once desirable may not be tomorrow.

The point is that your need to be dynamic might not necessarily be driven by a nimble company, a new app, or some whiz-bang technology. It could be the result of economic and societal shifts that impact the buying decisions of your customers. What was once desirable may not be tomorrow.

And often there is a ripple effect. What's the impact of autonomous vehicles on the insurance industry? When we have truly self-driving cars, will everyone still own a vehicle, or will people simply have one "delivered" to their house when needed? What's the impact of this on the parking garage business? The automotive industry in general? What about banks that rely on selling car loans? Many industries will

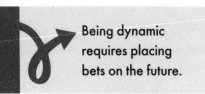

Being dynamic requires placing bets on the future.

be impacted, and you must be ready to adapt.

Being dynamic requires placing bets on the future. This can be risky and unpredictable. With the planted foot, given you have a long history of insights and information, you know where to double down and go deep. Therefore, placing big bets can be relatively safe. However, for the moving foot, we are in unknown territory. Our past won't inform our decisions as clearly. Therefore, you want to be more cautious with your investments. Where there is a higher level of uncertainty, you want to place a larger number of smaller bets. Experimentation and iterative development can be useful tools for mitigating risk because the future is unknown.

Predicting the Future

Being dynamic is not an intrinsic element of your differentiator but rather reflects changes in the market. It is related to whether the capability would stand the test of time.

The goal is to make sure that what you offer today continues to be valuable and desirable tomorrow. How can we see where we need to pivot when the future is uncertain? It's not easy to distinguish a fad from a trend.

For a while, plant-based alternative meats appeared to be the next hot trend, as they experienced a 45 percent growth in 2020 and became a billion-dollar industry. However, in 2021, sales were flat, and they trended downward in 2022. Declining consumer sentiment impacted sales, and inflation further exacerbated the situation due to the premium pricing of plant-based alternatives. This doesn't imply that it was a fad. It may just mean that the sustained growth trajectories might not be as significant as people initially anticipated.

And sometimes something that is wildly popular can end up being a fad. When introduced in 2013, Google Glass seemed poised to be the next big thing. However, concerns about privacy, high costs, and limited functionality led to waning interest, and Google discontinued the product for consumers in 2015. Similarly, the Segway Personal Transporter, introduced in 2001, was a self-balancing electric scooter that promised to revolutionize personal transportation. Despite the initial hype, high costs, safety concerns, and limited practicality rendered it a niche product and a fad. Pokémon Go also quickly attracted millions of users but lost its popularity within a few short months. And for those old enough to remember, the pet rocks craze was fortunately just a fad.

This book is not about predicting the future. There are many other resources where you can go to get that information. You can read up on scenario-based planning. You can partner with universities or organizations that follow trends. One effective strategy is to build a community of your top suppliers (rather than just customers) to understand what they are creating, as this gives insights into future capabilities that will be released.

Regardless, there is one difference between past-based decisions and prediction-based decisions: the level of uncertainty. When addressing the need to be dynamic (the moving foot), learning to place small bets can help you reduce the risk associated with uncertainty.

> The difference between past-based decisions and prediction-based decisions: the level of uncertainty. When addressing the need to be dynamic (the moving foot), learning to place small bets can help you reduce the risk associated with uncertainty.

Think Big, Start Small, Test Often

In June 1999, a website called ShoeSite.com was launched. Shortly after, they rebranded it to Zappos. They wanted to become the world's largest shoe store—and they achieved that goal. However, they didn't start there.

Think about this for a moment. If you're going to launch an online shoe store from scratch, what do you need? Maybe you need to build a warehouse. You might need to invest in a distribution network. And you might have to buy thousands of shoes to get started. Doing this would be a massive undertaking. And it would be risky. Remember, this was 1999, before the internet had fully taken over the world.

They didn't know if anybody would want to buy shoes on the internet. Given this, it would be a bad move to make huge bets and have it fail miserably. What did Zappos do instead?

Rather than assuming that the market wanted to buy shoes online, they did some simple and low-cost experiments. Instead of placing big bets, they placed small ones. They went to local retail shoe stores and took pictures of the shoes. They put them online and promoted the Zappos website to see if anybody wanted to buy shoes online. If no one bought, it was very little risk. And when someone did buy, Zappos would send one of their employees to the local shoe store, buy it at full retail price, package it up by hand, and stick it in the mail.

Clearly, they were losing money, and this approach wasn't sustainable. However, it served as an important test to determine the idea's viability. The initial tests were so successful that they continued to scale the concept. Initially, Zappos acted as an intermediary, collecting orders while others fulfilled them. Around 2004, they decided to bring warehouse and distribution in-house, a logical pivot after years of validation. This strategy proved successful, as Amazon acquired Zappos for $1.2 billion in 2009, and it continues to operate as a thriving business today.

When the future is unpredictable, instead of placing big bets, try small experiments.

SUMMARY: You Can Only Be Pivotal If You Know When to Pivot

The key to remaining desirable in the future is to first establish a strong foundation, and then, when necessary, pivot from a position of strength. Being anchored allows you to be nimble and adaptable without dissipating your energies. This is what it means to be dynamic.

Change should be built on a solid foundation, like a house. Once the house is built, you can redecorate and renovate or even add an addition. However, you would rarely tear the house down and start over. For many organizations, constant ungrounded pivoting is more like demolition than renovation.

You want to be dynamic, but ideally, you want to continue to build on a solid foundation. To be dynamic, remember to do the following:

- Consider technologies that might be disruptive to your business or industry. What is the impact of AI, blockchain, 3D printing, autonomous electric vehicles, or the metaverse on what you do? What if, instead of looking at these as disruptors, you looked at them as enablers to expand on your differentiator?
- Keep an eye open for shifting buyer behaviors. Just because customers flocked to you in the past doesn't mean the next generation will. What do they want that might be different from what you have offered in the past?
- When looking toward the future, instead of making large bets that might fail, experiment by placing smaller bets throughout the process. What's a small experiment

you could try today? How could you get everyone in your organization to conduct small, scalable experiments that take almost no time or money?
- While doing this, try to distinguish trends from fads. Partner with others who specialize in predicting the future. Look to universities, trend watchers, and even your suppliers.

> Being dynamic, nimble, and adaptable is important. You will need to change as the world evolves. You will need to pivot to remain desirable. But remember that being pivotal means pivoting from a place of power.

Being dynamic, nimble, and adaptable is important. You will need to change as the world evolves. You will need to pivot to remain desirable. But remember that being pivotal means pivoting from a place of power. Once you have a solid foundation that can support focused and purposeful change, you are able to scale. This leads us to the last D: Disseminated. This dimension is broken into two pieces: disseminated internally and disseminated externally.

Leverage

CHAPTER 10

Disseminated Internally

How Can You Scale Your Differentiator?

Don't Let Your Differentiator Be a Best-Kept Secret

When you apply the first four Ds, you will have a differentiator that is distinctive and desirable today and for the foreseeable future. It will stand the test of time in that it is difficult to replicate and is dynamic. Now, the question is, "How can you leverage your differentiator?"

As discussed in the section on the Innovation Targeting Matrix, there are a number of strategies for maximizing the impact of your support, core, and differentiating capabilities.

In this last D, we talk about how to get the word out to everyone. In other words, disseminate your differentiator. This needs to happen both internally and externally—with employees, customers, and business partners. When you pull this together, you end up with a very powerful framework for prioritizing your investments, collaborating with customers and suppliers, and maximizing the impact of every

> It is commonplace in business to say that "innovation is everyone's responsibility." It is. However, this sentiment often leads individuals to innovate everywhere, even in areas of the business that are low-value and non-differentiating. This detracts from the bottom line as it is wildly inefficient.

employee. Even if you nail the first four Ds, if you don't leverage them, you will never be pivotal.

It is critical to first disseminate the information internally so that everyone in your organization knows how they contribute to your differentiator. When it becomes an expression of everyone's daily work, people will live and breathe your differentiator, making it a reality.

In the next chapter, we discuss some powerful strategies for sharing your differentiator externally. Although it is helpful for developing sales and marketing strategies, the real value is in leveraging it as a tool to go deeper with your customers.

But first, let's look at how you can create a culture focused on differentiation.

Leveraging Your Differentiator Internally

It is commonplace in the business world to say that "innovation is everyone's responsibility." It is. However, this sentiment often leads individuals to innovate everywhere, even in areas of the business that are low-value and non-differentiating. This detracts from the bottom line as it is wildly inefficient. Instead, it's essential to ensure everyone understands your unique differentiator so that they can prioritize their tasks and focus on what matters most. Each person contributes to your differentiator, and it's crucial they understand how—not just intellectually but with a profound emotional connection. Each employee should feel pivotal to the company's success. This is what it means to disseminate your differentiator internally.

To make sure that everyone in your organization has a solid grasp of your differentiator, you need to find ways of gaining alignment. It's much more than having a poster that articulates your differentiator in as few words as possible. And it is also not achieved through new detailed policies and practices. The key is for everyone to have a deep understanding of your differentiator, combined with the mindset and tools to make it a reality. It's about everyone living and breathing your differentiator.

> Each person contributes to your differentiator, and it's crucial they understand how—not just intellectually but with a profound emotional connection. Each employee should feel pivotal to the company's success.

For insights on how to do this, we turn to language.

The Power of Linguistics When Communicating Your Differentiator

In linguistics, there is the concept of "deep" versus "surface" structure. The terms were coined by Noam Chomsky back in the 1960s and are relevant to business.

The deep structure is the meaning, what you want to convey; the surface structure is the actual configuration of words used to express what you want to say.

When you debate the specific words that should be used in articulating your differentiator (or even your mission or vision statement), you are automatically focusing on the surface structure. But if your goal is alignment and understanding, the words are not as important as the intent: the deep structure.

> When you debate the specific words that should be used in articulating your differentiator (or even your mission or vision statement), you are automatically focusing on the surface structure. But if your goal is alignment and understanding, the words are not as important as the intent: the deep structure.

Access to the deep structure is not intellectual. It is visceral. How do you do this? Generate emotion. Find ways to communicate your differentiator so that it speaks to people at a deeper level.

Visit and interview customers and clients. Talk to individuals and organizations that have been impacted by your work. Talk with employees, partners, vendors, or anyone who might have some great gut-level reactions to your differentiator, and have them share personal stories. Sharing these stories is the best way for people to get your differentiator in their souls. This is exactly what Radio Flyer did when they discovered they weren't in the wagon business but rather in the business of bringing smiles and creating warm memories that last a lifetime. Their differentiator—and their soul—was discovered in the stories.

The specific wording of your differentiator (the surface structure) is not as important as the meaning behind the words (the deep structure). This is where you tap into implicit motivations.

This concept of deep versus surface structure also applies to your business model. Companies are known for having binders of policies, practices, and processes. The goal is to ensure some level of consistency. However, these documents typically only describe the surface structure, how the work should be done. What really needs to be conveyed is the deep structure behind these policies and processes. To begin to do this, you will want to start with some questions: Why are they designed this way? What do we want to achieve? What is the impact of doing things this way? Why are we in business?

The "why" and "what" are about the deep structure. You want people to grasp this beyond just an intellectual level. You want everyone to have a profound understanding of it. Unfortunately, in an effort to disseminate their strategies, most businesses document the "how": the surface structure. And the little deep structure that is provided is given at an intellectual level. Doing this limits innovation ... and true self-expression.

Is Your Business Designed like Classical Music or Jazz?

Music provides an apt metaphor to illustrate the difference between surface and deep structures and their impact on business operations. It provides insight into how to disseminate your differentiator.

Classical music is an example of surface structure. There is very little room for interpretation. With little variation, different orchestras play a given composition in very similar ways. Jazz, on the other hand, is often about the deep structure: the chords, rhythm, and time signature. Armed with this information, a jazz ensemble can improvise and innovate within the confines of this intention, rather than being forced to play a specific set of notes. The players are free to express what comes to them in the moment while adhering to the imposed guidelines.

Businesses, like jazz ensembles, need simple structures to foster innovation to emerge. They need a set of

> Businesses, like jazz ensembles, need simple structures that foster innovation. They need a set of principles that help everyone deliver on their differentiator.

principles that help everyone deliver on their differentiator. But jazz is much more than just improvisation. It is the fruit of the activity of a group of people. Jazz is a social activity, and so are businesses.

At a conference in France, I illustrated the connection between jazz improvisation and business innovation. After discussing adaptability in business, I brought out a group of jazz musicians I'd commissioned but never met. Grabbing my tenor sax, I simply told them, "Twelve-bar B-flat blues." We dove in, delivering fifteen minutes of spontaneous music. I believe the audience grasped the concept. To showcase a traditional approach, I'd have picked up my bassoon and played a classical piece without deviation. Sadly, many businesses operate more like orchestras than like jazz bands. We ask people to do rote tasks instead of letting them think of better ways to do their work. If you want to see a snippet of the speech where I played the sax, you can find the video on the tools page I previously mentioned:

www.ThePivotalTools.com

When organizations focus on the deep structure, improvisation begins to emerge. Innovation becomes a more natural act because everyone is clear on the "why" and "what." From there, they can innovate the "how." Work becomes a truer expression of each individual yet is aligned with the differentiator. With this, creativity emerges from everyone within the structure.

Just as I was able to create jazz music in France without any preparation or an elaborate musical score, a business can rapidly disseminate the differentiator when it focuses on the deep structure—the meaning behind your differentiator.

Create Structures to Disseminate

Once you have defined the deep structure of your differentiator, it is time to disseminate it widely. This needs to be more than simply sharing the concepts behind your differentiator. You want people to experience it.

This widespread dissemination was a challenge I faced in 1996 while working for Accenture (then Andersen Consulting). I was tasked with developing an innovation mindset within the company. It wasn't about training in detailed processes but rather fundamental principles that described the way we needed to operate. This was our set of differentiators.

The strategy we employed enabled us to put twenty thousand consultants through our one-day program, which provided them with a firsthand experience of the principles. We completed this first phase within nine months. The impact of disseminating our differentiator this way proved to provide a sustained impact for the organization, as we created structures that provided support long after their session.

Our strategy revolved around a blend of top-down and bottom-up approaches. First, let's explore the organizational hierarchy, which consisted of the following:

Leadership: Top leaders must be aligned with the overarching goals and strategy.

Masters: A select group of individuals who mastered the differentiators and acted as the primary mentors.

Ambassadors: Although they didn't have the same depth of understanding or experience with the differentiators, they played a crucial role in disseminating the content.

Extended Network: The broader organization with varying levels of engagement.

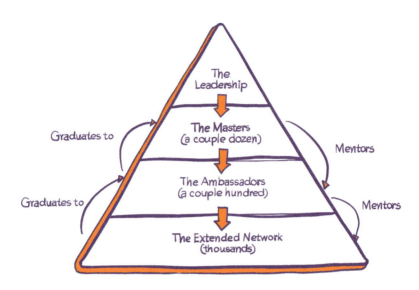

To successfully shift the culture and disseminate our differentiator (and associated principles), specific steps were essential:

STEP 1: DEVELOP THE DELIVERY PLAN

Success metrics were clear from the start. What would success look like? How would it be measured? Although success was partly measured by education, the real impact was from application, value creation, and sustainability. How can we create more value for our clients so that they want to keep on working with us? How can we continue to innovate where we differentiate?

STEP 2: BUILD THE CORE TEAM AND DEVELOP THE CONTENT

Once we were clear on what we wanted to achieve and the leadership was bought in, it was time to build a small core team. These were the "Masters." They would become experts in our principles, the process, and our differentiators.

We initially started with a group of six individuals dedicated to the task of creating materials that would share our principles and differentiators throughout the company. We developed a one-day experiential program, a book with the principles, and a quick reference card that summarized everything. Over time, we expanded the team of Masters to a couple dozen people by adding individuals who weren't completely dedicated to our work, as they had other full-time roles. They served as the primary point of contact for the Ambassadors, as the Masters were the individuals with the deepest level of expertise. Armed with these materials, we were ready to start disseminating.

STEP 3: SELECT AND TRAIN THE AMBASSADORS

Next, we selected two hundred consultants, approximately 1 percent of our organization, to serve as Ambassadors. These individuals were passionate about our work and eager to share our principles, as these consultants were already exemplifying our differentiators. With the assistance of the Masters, these two hundred Ambassadors attended a three-day train-the-trainer workshop to ensure consistent training delivery worldwide.

STEP 4: ROLL OUT

After equipping the Masters and Ambassadors with the necessary materials, they jointly delivered over 250 full-day sessions worldwide. Trainers teamed up, with each committing to conduct multiple sessions organized by geography, department, or line of business.

STEP 5: CREATE SUPPORT STRUCTURES

We knew that a daylong program would have little long-term impact if it weren't backed up by other materials. Therefore, in addition to the program, we created a book, a pocket guide, and an online library. More importantly, we established vital support communities that included the Masters Network, the Ambassadors Network, and a Community of Interest. These formal groups ensured continuous conversation, engagement, and skill enhancement.

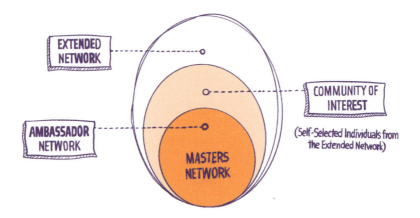

A significant aspect of the model was that, besides mentoring the lower levels of the pyramid, individuals could advance to higher levels. We recognized and rewarded those who took the initiative to improve the organization and shared their knowledge. This kept the model fresh for many years.

In fact, the lasting impact of the program was evident five years after its initial delivery. It wasn't just a training exercise but a significant cultural shift. Even as our differentiators evolved, the supporting structures facilitated continuous sharing and dissemination. Changes could be propagated throughout the organization repeatedly and rapidly. The pyramid model is one I have replicated many times with great success across a wide range of companies in various industries and of different sizes.

SUMMARY: How to Be Pivotal by Disseminating and Leveraging Your Differentiator Internally

To be pivotal, you need to ensure that everyone in your organization knows how they are pivotal to your organization's success. To get the most from your talent, disseminate internally.

Ensure that everyone knows your differentiator, not just intellectually but viscerally. It's not about people being able to recite slogans. It's about everyone understanding how they contribute to the organization's success—and living it each and every day.

- *Focus on the deep structure*: To have the greatest impact with internal communications, avoid looking for slogans you can post on walls. How can you ensure everyone has a visceral understanding of what matters to the organization? How can you help them understand how their contributions matter? Focus on the deep structure of your communications, not just the surface structure.
- *Design like jazz*: In addition to communication, it's also essential to have the right level of structures and processes. Instead of prescriptive procedural manuals, how can you give employees the flexibility to innovate during the moments when it matters most? Instead of elaborate compositions like classical music, strive for streamlined organization models that are more like jazz.
- *Create structures*: Once your messages are set and your organization models are designed, it's time to create supporting structures. Form a small core team of

> **Once everyone internally is playing the same music, it is time to bring it to the rest of the world and leverage it externally.**

Masters who possess a deep understanding of your unique differentiators and supporting capabilities. These individuals will mentor the Ambassadors, who will then assist the rest of the organization. Also, create communities and communication mechanisms so that the concepts stay alive, are continually shared, and can evolve as your differentiator shifts.

Leveraging your differentiator internally is critical. Everyone needs to understand how they are pivotal to the success of your organization.

Once everyone internally is playing the same music, it is time to bring it to the rest of the world and leverage it externally.

CHAPTER 11

Disseminated Externally

How Can You Sell Your Differentiator?

Sell Where You Differentiate

At the end of the day, although you can declare your differentiator, buyers will ultimately determine its value with their wallets. When you ask customers "Why do you do business with us and not the competition?," they should be able to articulate the differentiator you are focused on. Therefore, it is critical that you share your differentiator externally in an authentic way.

One company that has done this particularly well is Westin. I've worked with the hotel industry for many years, and when I would ask people on the street, "Which hotel chain has the best beds?," a large percentage would say, "Westin." Why? Because back in 1999, Westin launched, trademarked, and branded the Heavenly Bed. Prior to that time, most hotel beds were foam-based mattresses designed less for comfort and more for budget-friendliness. When guests were asked what was the most important service a hotel could offer, their answer was, "A good night's sleep." Westin spent over a year researching the best mattress options, invested $50 million in upgrading rooms, and spent countless dollars on marketing campaigns. At the time, there was no competition, and they made sure they got that message out to the world.

> Make sure your company's differentiator is not a best-kept secret. Although we've talked extensively about the need to innovate where you differentiate, it is also important to sell (market, communicate, etc.) where you differentiate.

Make sure your company's differentiator is not a best-kept secret. Although we've talked extensively about the need to innovate where you differentiate, it is also important to *sell* (market, communicate, etc.) where you differentiate.

This concept applies to even the most commoditized products, such as toothpaste. If your advertisements simply state, "We reduce cavities and freshen breath," you'd better be the least expensive option. However, to be a premium product, you need to sell and market where you differentiate. For example, Crest Pro-Health advertises itself as the only toothpaste that provides protection against cavities, gingivitis, plaque, sensitive teeth, and tartar buildup while freshening breath and whitening teeth. Tom's of Maine, on the other hand, markets itself as a natural toothpaste that uses organic, sustainable, and environmentally friendly ingredients, with fluoride derived from natural sources like tea leaves and oyster shells. Sensodyne has built its name and brand around reducing tooth sensitivity and strengthening enamel, and Arm & Hammer focuses on its use of baking soda to neutralize acids and freshen breath as part of its marketing strategy. Rather than selling the core benefits, such as reducing cavities, which are expected from all toothpaste brands, it's important to focus on how you differentiate yourself in the market.

Help Your Customers Innovate Where They Differentiate

Sometimes the best way to sell where you differentiate is to learn how your customers differentiate.

One aspect of my differentiator is the fact that I've spent over twenty-five years in the field of corporate innovation and led a twenty-thousand-person process and innovation practice at Accenture. I have pretty much dedicated my career to studying and applying the latest and greatest thinking in this area.

For my clients, innovation is critical, but it is core. The application of innovation techniques might help them differentiate, but staying on top of the latest innovation trends might be a distraction. This is why clients work with me. I help them with innovation so that they can do what they do best.

> Sometimes the best way to sell where you differentiate is to learn how your customers differentiate.

In my view, this section could prove to be the most valuable section for the right reader, offering strategies to maximize value creation for your customers. This is especially relevant for business-to-business (B2B) organizations, such as parts manufacturers that supply other companies or service providers that assist businesses. These principles will also be useful for departments that serve internal customers or those engaged in external partnerships. In fact, with a dose of creative thinking, the insights presented here can be adapted to virtually any business scenario.

Remember the ITM from section 2? You may recall that there are three levels of activities: support, core, and differentiating. So far, we have only talked about how you use that internally to prioritize investments. Now we will show you how you can use this model to get your customers to prioritize *their* investments so that they will find you even more valuable. This is the most powerful way to be truly pivotal to their business.

When you handle the core or support aspects of your customer's business, you allow them to focus on what is most important. In other words, you enable them to innovate where *they* differentiate.

Find Your Customers' Differentiators

The concept is simple yet powerful. When you can understand what is support and core for your customers, you can look at how your differentiator can take those tasks off their plates.

I was working with a group of maintenance companies specializing in supporting heating, ventilation, and air-conditioning systems for commercial buildings. The leaders of their organizations were struggling to figure out how to differentiate. When we talked about how their differentiator can help their clients focus on their own differentiator, the lightbulb went on.

> When you understand what is support and core for your customers, look at how your differentiator can take those tasks off their plates.

Imagine sitting with your client and you bring out the ITM. You ask them to consider what work they do that is differentiating. What is most important to *their* customers? Then you have them list the activities they do that are support and core. Now tell them that these activities are a distraction and prevent them from focusing on what matters most.

Now bring out your list of differentiators. How can your differentiators help your customers stop worrying about critical yet core activities, thus freeing them to focus on their differentiator?

Manage Your Customers' Core to Enable Their Differentiation

An insightful example from my time with Dr. Michael Hammer, the pioneer of business reengineering and author of *Reengineering the Corporation*, illustrates the power of using your differentiator to help customers focus less on *their* core and more on their differentiators. Navistar, a bus and truck manufacturer, used to manage its own tire-and-rim inventory at its Ohio assembly plant. But for them, this was only core. Their primary differentiator was the manufacturing of buses and trucks.

Leverage your distinctive capabilities to help others focus on theirs.

When Goodyear, one of Navistar's suppliers, offered to take over the tire warehouse, it was a win-win situation. By electronically accessing Navistar's manufacturing details, Goodyear prepared the tire-and-rim assemblies at its own plant and timed the delivery to Navistar's perfectly, aligning with the finished trucks rolling off the assembly line. This completely eliminated the inventory at Navistar's tire warehouse.

Because of Goodyear's expertise, inventory days of tires and rims were reduced from twenty-two to just five. For Goodyear, tire warehousing was a differentiator; for Navistar, it was only core. Handing over tire warehouse management to Goodyear freed Navistar to focus on its differentiator of truck and bus manufacturing. This strategic move let each company play to its strengths.

Earlier in the book, we explored how CCC handled the core activity of claims processing so that the major insurance companies could focus on their differentiators. These are powerful examples of how to sell where you differentiate. You leverage your distinctive capabilities to help others so they can focus on theirs. There are a few other ways you can leverage this "sell where you differentiate" model to help others focus on their differentiator. Let's take a look.

Support Your Customers' Support Activities

Maybe your differentiator solves a support problem for your customers. If so, this would make you a fantastic outsourcing provider. What you offer doesn't necessarily create value for your customers' customers, but it certainly creates value for *your* customers. Every company needs a payroll system. Although paying employees is not core or differentiating for most companies, it is important. And from a volume perspective, there are nearly an unlimited number of companies that want these services. So it might be a volume game rather than a value game. But it can be highly profitable.

A midsized bank in Canada had a clever strategy they used many years ago. They realized that they had an excellent procurement process, especially as it related to office supplies. Although this is support for them, they realized it had the potential to do much more. Because of their scale and efficiencies, they could purchase common business items for a fraction of the retail cost.

> Maybe your differentiator solves a support problem for your customers. If so, this would make you a fantastic outsourcing provider.

These are standard office supplies such as paper, toner, and furniture. One of their target markets were smaller businesses. These customers were often paying full retail for these items because they didn't have any purchasing power. What did the bank do? It offered office supplies at wholesale rates to its customers as a way of attracting and keeping them. What was support for the bank eventually became a differentiator in that no one else was offering this service to small businesses.

Sell to Your Internal Customers

There are times when disseminating externally actually means communicating with people within your company who are your internal customers.

I worked with a major food manufacturer for over a year. A couple dozen employees went through one of my programs. We covered a wide range of innovation topics over the twelve months.

When it came to the conversation around differentiation, many on the team struggled at first. A common question was, "Isn't our differentiator something that is determined by senior leadership? If so, why are we spending time learning it?" The answer is that the 5Ds and the ITM are valuable at every level of the organization, just in different ways (note: in section 4, we cover how to apply the concepts to employees, entrepreneurs, and others).

At this organization, we explored how to use these tools to make their internal customers aware of their capabilities. The department in question was a research group that analyzed a wide variety of compounds. One of their groups was located so far away from the headquarters that they

> There are times when disseminating externally actually means communicating with people within your company who are your internal customers.

> Selling where you differentiate to internal customers can be critical for clarifying how your group is pivotal.

were nearly forgotten. In addition, there were other departments in the company that also performed analytical work. With so many analytical groups, the question was sometimes raised by higher-ups in the organization as to why each existed.

As part of our work together, the department I was working with realized that they needed to do a better job of communicating with others about their differentiator. Unfortunately, all the groups were lumped together into the same category of analysis. If they didn't clearly articulate their differentiator and their reason for existence, it would be easy enough for them to be eliminated.

As it turns out, each group does indeed bring a distinctive capability that is critical. One group's differentiator was that it could analyze samples without knowing what was in them. Other groups could analyze samples only when they knew what they contained but could go deeper with the analysis. Each brought something different to the table. They figured out a way to communicate how they were pivotal to the overall success of the company. The takeaway here is that selling where you differentiate to internal customers can be critical for clarifying how your group is pivotal.

Invest in Your Suppliers

This concept also applies to others in your value chain—not just customers. How can you assist in solving your suppliers' problems? How could that be valuable to them and you? How can you be pivotal to their success?

Years ago I worked with a major potato chip manufacturer whose critical suppliers were the small businesses that grew potatoes.

Think about how most manufacturers or retailers treat their suppliers and vendors. The typical approach is to squeeze the heck out of them, forcing the suppliers to cut their costs and adhere to the larger company's rules. Although this might work in the short run, it builds an adversarial relationship between the companies.

> This concept also applies to others in your value chain—not just customers. How can you assist in solving your suppliers' problems? How could that be valuable to them and you? How can you be pivotal to their success?

And in the case of independent farmers who grow potatoes, it could put them out of business. Margins are thin enough as it is.

So what did this snack food company do? They asked themselves, "What can we do on behalf of the family farmers to help them?" Instead of squeezing them, they decided to "invest" in the potato growers. They leveraged their scale and reach to help the growers acquire the necessary equipment at a reduced cost. They educated the growers on techniques that would increase their crop yields. They provided products and services to their suppliers to help them be more successful. Nothing was expected in return. The growers were not forced to offer preferred rates. They were not forced into exclusive arrangements. But at the end of the day, the farmers were always going to find ways to repay their customer. Moral of the story: investing in your vendors can pay dividends.

Although this example doesn't explicitly use the ITM, the concept is the same. Leverage a strength of yours to help others in ways that they might not be able to do for themselves.

SUMMARY: How to Be Pivotal by Disseminating and Leveraging Your Differentiator Externally

Being pivotal requires that your target market knows and values your differentiator. There are several strategies for doing this and making the greatest impact:

- *Market and sell where you differentiate.* Look at your marketing materials and sales pitches. How much time do you spend on core messages versus those that are truly differentiating? During sales conversations, your core represents only the basic expectations of your customers. Instead, focus on what makes you special. What do you do better than anyone else that they would value?
- *Help your customers innovate where* they *differentiate.* When you have clarity on what is core and support for your customers, you can engage in powerful conversations about how your work will free them to focus on what is most important to them. Using the ITM as a customer conversation starter can help kick-start the process.
- *Take over your customers' core activities.* You can help your customers focus on their differentiators by handling their core tasks using your differentiators. This helps them to zero in on what's most important.
- *Take over your customers' support activities.* Your customers' support activities need to run efficiently. By taking that work off their plates, you enable them to redirect their efforts toward crucial differentiating work.
- *Sell to your internal customers.* To be pivotal inside your organization, your team must sell where you

differentiate to internal customers. Focus on your most distinctive and desirable capabilities.
- *Invest in your suppliers.* Instead of squeezing your suppliers out of business, find ways to help them be more successful. When you are pivotal to their success, they will be sure to find ways of being pivotal to *your* success.

SECTION FOUR

Beyond the Organization

CHAPTER 12

It's About the Individual

Applying Differentiation Beyond the Four Walls

I remember speaking with a client who went through one of my programs. He was a midlevel manager running a small team. At first he struggled with the topic of differentiation. He asked, "How does this apply to me when the top executives make all the big decisions?" Yes, the leaders might make some of the macro-level decisions on differentiation, but it needs to cascade down.

I asked him, "How does your team differentiate itself? How do you offer something to your internal customers that no one else can?" Using this mindset, he was able to guide the team through the process of prioritizing their

> For some, the real value goes beyond the organization level, but is about how they can differentiate as an individual.

> **If you want to be pivotal in your career, you must master the power of differentiation. If you want to create the greatest impact and stand out in a competitive workplace, learn where to plant your feet to get the most traction.**

investments based on the department's differentiator.

But for him, the real value went beyond the organization; it was about how he as an individual could differentiate. He asked, "How do I differentiate myself from other employees in the company?" This was a lightbulb moment for him and shifted his relationship to the content.

When I work with clients on the concepts shared in this book, many immediately assume that this work is for the C-suite only. But hopefully, by now, you've seen how it applies at every level of an organization.

If you want to be pivotal in your career, you must master the power of differentiation. If you want to create the greatest impact so you can stand out in a competitive workplace, learn where to plant your feet to get the most traction.

Here's the reality. Differentiation is a multifaceted process that addresses the outside world, customers, internal culture, team behavior, and other forces. But at the end of the day, it all comes down to you. You need to be pivotal to the organization through your unique capabilities.

You, the individual, need to learn, live, and breathe the concepts in this book. Apply them everywhere. And then find ways of collaborating with others around *their* differentiators. One person can make a meaningful difference, but the biggest impact is when others are speaking the same language and there is alignment in the thinking and approach.

This section is about how these concepts can be applied to you as an individual, regardless of your current career situation, whether you are an employee, a solopreneur (someone who has their own business without any other employees), an entrepreneur, a freelancer, or maybe you don't have a traditional job. It doesn't matter. The concepts are universal. Anyone can use them anywhere.

We explore three different ways to look at the 5Ds: for employees, for entrepreneurs, and for our personal lives. I find myself using the frameworks and perspectives in this book daily. It helps me stay grounded and gives me clarity on what I am doing and where I am going.

For your differentiator to be valuable to you as an individual, it also has to be valuable to others. This is the desirable aspect. It has to be something you love doing (internal desirability), and it must be something others need or want (external desirability). And in some cases, what makes you special needs to also be durable, dynamic, and disseminated.

> For your differentiator to be valuable to you as an individual, it also has to be valuable to others. This is the desirable aspect. It has to be something you love doing (internal desirability), and it must be something others need or want (external desirability). What makes you special also needs to be distinctive, durable, dynamic, and disseminated.

CHAPTER 13

Differentiation for Employees

Differentiation on the Job

Maybe you have a job and you work for someone else. In this situation, your differentiator will be critical for your career advancement, assuming that's something you desire.

As an employee, you want to make distinctive, special contributions. To be clear, this doesn't mean you have to be the best in one particular area. It is the combination of various attributes that you bring to the table. Indeed, it might be the skills you were hired for, but it could also be your hobbies, personality, work ethic, or life experiences. These factors, when combined, make you unique. And when combined in the right way, they will make you distinctive.

It doesn't mean you have to be an expert. In fact, sometimes it is valuable not to have expertise. By looking at a problem with fresh eyes, you might offer perspectives that no one else has. Alternatively, you may possess a truly exceptional work ethic, organizational abilities,

> As an employee, you want to make distinctive contributions. This doesn't mean you have to be the best in one particular area. It is the combination of various attributes that you bring to the table.

or communication skills. All of these combined make you distinctive. But that's not enough. You need the desirable element—both internally and externally.

From an internal perspective, you have to enjoy what you are doing. You must desire the work, otherwise you will get bored or burned out. But you also need external desirability. If, for example, music is one of your hobbies, how can that make you more desirable? If you are a computer programmer, perhaps the way you compose music helps you write code that is easier to maintain. Or, as was the case with a potato chip manufacturer, a bass player discovered a way to remove excess fat from chips using sound waves. This innovative technique resulted in lower-fat chips that maintained their original form, unlike other methods that often crushed the chips into crumbs. Connect your distinctiveness and interests to what others want and need. Let's now turn to durable and dynamic.

Is what you offer today something that others can't copy? Given it is your life experience, it is probably somewhat unique to you. But will it truly stand the test of time? While writing this book, Apple announced that it will offer a technology to convert books into audiobooks using AI. Will this put voice narrators out of business? Possibly. Or maybe it changes the game. Maybe it means that the best ones will rise to the top because computers can never fully replace them, while the ones who are amateurs need to find a different profession—or up their game. According to a Goldman Sachs report, other AI tools like ChatGPT have the potential to impact up to three hundred million jobs. However, it's unlikely that most jobs will be completely replaced by AI. Instead, those who learn how to effectively use these powerful tools will have a competitive advantage. To stay relevant in the future, individuals may need to supplement their own skills and experience with AI-based tools. This requires a dynamic approach to learning and adapting to new technologies.

Let's face it, we should always be upping our game. With remote work, anyone around the world can be hired by any company. In some countries, individuals will gladly work for a fraction of what you charge. Keep your eye on your value today and tomorrow.

> **If you are an employee, get clear on your differentiator and how it can create value for the organization. How can you best contribute to the organization's success? And how can you communicate that to others so that team members and leaders know how to best leverage your talents?**

Finally, we get to the last D: Disseminated. If you are the world's best-kept secret, it might not bode well for you in the long run. I'm not suggesting you boast all the time. But make sure people are aware of your work. Make sure your value is understood. You don't need to share everything you do. But "share where you differentiate." What makes you special is what people need to understand. It is about communication. You want to position yourself as pivotal to the company's success.

SUMMARY: You Are Pivotal as an Employee

The concepts in this book apply to you as an individual. For you to make the greatest impact and be as successful as possible, you need to understand how *you* are pivotal.

If you are an employee, get clear on your differentiator and how it can create value for the organization. How can you best contribute to the organization's success? And how can you communicate that to others so that team members and leaders know how to best leverage your talents?

CHAPTER 14

Differentiation for Entrepreneurs

Differentiation When You Don't Work for Someone Else

What if you own your own business? It could be a small company, or perhaps you are a solopreneur. Alternatively, you might be a freelancer or gig worker. How do these concepts apply? Pretty much the same as for any organization. But getting clarity is even more important. Because you probably don't have the big budgets or resources of your larger competitor, prioritization is critical. Therefore, it is important to get clear on your differentiator.

Your differentiator not only needs to be distinctive, but it also needs to be desirable. It's not uncommon for entrepreneurs to launch businesses that interest them (internal desirability). However, if you rely solely on the idea of "do what you love, and the money will follow," you might end up broke. External desirability is crucial since your buyers must value what you offer. And, of course, don't forget to focus on differentiators that are durable and dynamic.

Clarifying and leveraging my differentiator is something I think about regularly as an entrepreneur. Getting this right helps me stay focused and avoid distractions.

Just as my clients find it helpful to bring in external support to help them find their differentiators, I, too, needed that outside perspective. I hired a branding agency that identified several differentiators that set me apart from others, and I use these regularly to prioritize my efforts.

Not surprisingly, my content, processes, and approaches are part of my differentiator. I aim to be provocative yet practical. But there's more to it than that. My personality is essential to clients, as surveys revealed they appreciate my sincerity, friendliness, and genuine concern for their needs. Clearly, this is something that can't be replicated or outsourced. I've also been told I am perceptive and can see problems, opportunities, and solutions that others can't. The final aspect of my differentiator is being impactful and caring about the results produced. It is the combination of all four that helps me stand out.

Examining my differentiator through the lens of the Ds, I believe it is distinctive, desirable, and durable. Beyond the first three Ds, I need to be aware of the dynamic dimension (for example, how AI will impact my ability to be desirable in the future or how economic conditions might impact demand for innovation investments) and ensure that I market and sell in areas where I differentiate (disseminate). Notice that none of the attributes of my differentiator are products or services. They are innate capabilities that can be leveraged to create many different offerings.

Once you have clarity on your differentiator, the ITM will be invaluable. You simply don't have the resources to do everything yourself. With limited time, it's crucial to delegate, eliminate, automate, partner, or outsource the right work. If everything is important, nothing will be done well.

I use the ITM by breaking down activities into smaller components and mapping them to support, core, and differentiating categories. This helps me prioritize tasks and determine which ones I should focus on or delegate.

> If you are an entrepreneur, it is critical to use the ITM to prioritize your time and money investments. How can you get others to handle your support and core work so that you can focus on your differentiator?

Although I am a nerd and enjoy goofing around with websites and technology, my clients don't hire me because I have the best website. It's not a differentiator. However, it is part of the client experience and therefore is core. I partner with others to ensure I have compelling copy, an aesthetic design, and 100 percent uptime. Websites and technology can be a fun distraction for me. Therefore, I need to keep reminding myself that they are not a differentiator.

The point is, the ITM, combined with clarity on your differentiator, can help you make better prioritization decisions and help you determine what you should eliminate or outsource. By becoming crystal clear on your differentiator, concentrating your efforts there, and hiring others to handle the rest, you will unleash higher levels of productivity and bring sanity to your business.

SUMMARY: You Are Pivotal as an Entrepreneur

If you are an entrepreneur, it is critical to use the ITM to help you prioritize your time and money investments. How can you get others to handle your support and core work so that you can focus on your differentiator?

CHAPTER 15

Differentiation in Your Personal Life

Applying the Concepts Every Day and Everywhere

In my earlier book, *Goal-Free Living: How to Have the Life You Want Now!*, I commissioned a study and discovered some intriguing statistics that suggest the life we live may not always be of our own choosing. One prompt in particular was quite telling: "I sometimes get the feeling that I am living my life in a way that satisfies others (friends, family, coworkers) more than it satisfies me."

More than 50 percent of the people surveyed said they either agreed or strongly agreed with that statement. At an individual level, often we choose to invest our time in endeavors that might not be our own.

Who we are in life is a function of all our past experiences. They shape and influence us. And in some cases, they can limit our ability to see the world with fresh eyes.

> More than 50 percent of the people surveyed agreed with the statement: "I sometimes get the feeling that I am living my life in a way that satisfies others (friends, family, coworkers) more than it satisfies me."

Applying the concept from this book to your personal life can help you uncover and utilize your innate gifts. This will enable you to identify areas where you excel and feel energized—something that truly ignites your passion and sets you apart from others. These abilities are not typically the ones you learned to be good at, as those often drain you of your energy. Rather, they are natural talents and strengths that you were born with.

To apply the concepts of this book to your personal life, first you must define what you want out of life. What do you enjoy doing? What brings you pleasure? What comes easily and instills a sense of peace? What sources of adventure do you find challenging yet invigorating? It's always a good idea to start with internal desirability. What are things you love doing that you are good at? This gets to distinctiveness. What is it that you do that makes you special? And if the outside world values what you do, even better. You can get great pleasure when your hobbies and passions turn into something social or maybe even profitable.

What is it that others desire? Perhaps it's finding collaborators who share your interests. It could be people who appreciate what you do, or it might be something of value that you offer, leading to others wanting to purchase from you.

Answering these questions can be difficult. If, like most people, you've lived according to the rules and desires of others, it might be challenging to view your life from a fresh perspective.

The key to discovering the answers to these questions is to have a broader set of life experiences. When describing why creative people are so, Steve Jobs once said, "They were able to connect experiences they've had and synthesize new things. And the reason they were able to do that was that they've had more experiences, or they have thought more about their experiences than other people."

To uncover your hidden differentiators, seek out new experiences. You will often find that the best ones aren't always on your to-do list. Therefore, introduce some flexibility into your life rather than planning every detail. Instead of a map, try using a compass.

Yes, maps can be useful. They provide the comfort we need to get from point A to point B as directly and efficiently as possible. However, life is not about efficiency; it's about exuberance. And you can't map out desire. Maps can become restrictive when we rely on them too heavily to guide our every move.

> To uncover your hidden differentiators, seek out new experiences. You will often find that the best ones aren't always on your to-do list. Therefore, introduce some flexibility into your life rather than planning every detail. Instead of a map, try using a compass.

The secret is to find a compass setting that moves you in a direction that feels right—an aspiration that is big, bold, and calls you to action. Seek something that inspires you. Instead of targeting a specific destination, find a sense of direction that draws you forward and then "meander with purpose." Try new things and venture into an unknown, uncharted, and unplanned future. Have the courage to change direction often, discovering new paths along the way. Choose paths that align with your dreams, hopes, and aspirations, as these form your compass. What did you enjoy

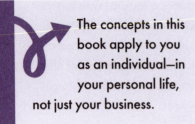

The concepts in this book apply to you as an individual—in your personal life, not just your business.

doing as a child? What have you often considered doing but dismissed due to a lack of time or money? What passion have you held in your heart, only to be discouraged by others who deemed it a crazy idea? Which hobby or interest could be transformed into a career? What would you do if money were not an issue?

Look deep inside yourself. Go beyond what you think you *should* be doing as a responsible adult, and find what you really *want* to do with your life.

Most people try to intellectualize what they want to do with their lives. They create spreadsheets with lists of pros and cons, likes and dislikes. They take classes and workshops where they sit and think about their life. But sometimes it is difficult to intellectualize what you truly desire. You have to experience it. Many people I meet say, "I would change careers if only I knew what to do." Without this sense of direction, they are stuck. How do you get unstuck? Get out and explore, try new things, meet new people—live your life through each experience.

When you do this, you will discover (and experience) activities that you like and ones that you do not like. Then use your desire as a barometer to help determine which direction to turn. Do more of the things that you like and less of the things that you don't.

SUMMARY: You Are Pivotal

The concepts in this book apply to you as an individual–in your personal life, not just your business. How can you blend internal desirability (something you love doing), external desirability (something the world values), and what makes you distinctive (your superpower)? If you want to dig deeper into the topic of "meandering with purpose," please read my book *Goal-Free Living*.

As mentioned in the introduction, *Pivotal* is about the first step of the FAST Innovation® model. It's about focusing on differentiating opportunities. The next chapter digs deeper into each step of the process.

FAST Innovation®

Accelerate the Way You Innovate

The book you just read focused on the strategic part of innovation. Where do we dig deep to provide a solid foundation for our business?

Although getting clarity around your differentiator starts as up-front work, it must be a living, breathing framework that is to be revisited and revised. It should be incorporated into new employee onboarding and used as a reference by everyone in the company. It should influence investment decisions and shape both internal and external communications. Ultimately, it should serve as a cornerstone of everything you do. Although it might be the first step of the innovation process, it needs to live on and be used continuously.

To help my clients accelerate the way they innovate, I developed my four-step FAST Innovation process.

FAST is an acronym that stands for the following:

- Focus—Focus on differentiators.
- Ask—Ask better questions.
- Shift—Shift perspectives to find hidden solutions.
- Test—Test, experiment, and implement solutions.

Focus

This book addressed the Focus step. Make sure you have clarity on your differentiator, and then innovate where you differentiate. With this focus, you can now start prioritizing your initiatives and targeting the biggest opportunities. The key to doing this is to know which questions to ask and how to ask them. This leads us to the second step of the FAST Innovation process.

Ask

Once you know where to focus your energies, it is time to identify the opportunities and challenges that need to be addressed. This is the "Ask" step.

I've written an entire book on this subject: *Invisible Solutions: 25 Lenses that Reframe and Help Solve Difficult Business Problems*. It contains twenty-five different lenses that reframe problems and opportunities in multiple ways. This process helps you see solutions that might otherwise remain hidden from view.

You can get your copy of *Invisible Solutions* here:
www.InvisibleSolutionsBook.com

Shift

Once you have well-framed and differentiating opportunities, it is time to find solutions. This is the "Shift" step.

When solving complex problems, our expertise often limits the range of solutions we might consider. Our answers are often based on past experience. This isn't necessarily bad, but it tends to lead to incremental innovation. In some cases, it might even prevent the finding of workable solutions. Compound this with the tendency of smart people to prioritize *being* right over *doing* what is right, and you're left with a limited range of options. To shift your perspective, you need to bring together people from a wide range of disciplines, backgrounds, and experiences.

> When solving complex problems, our expertise often limits the range of solutions we might consider. Our answers are often based on past experience.

If you are interested in learning more about the power of bringing together a diverse range of experiences and disciplines, please watch my six-minute TEDxNASA video at
www.ShapiroTEDx.com

Related to this is the diversity of personalities. Despite the common belief that opposites attract, scientific evidence strongly suggests otherwise. We gravitate toward those who mirror us, instinctively surrounding ourselves with like-minded individuals. However, this homogeneity can hinder our ability to shift perspectives. Consequently, aligning yourself with people who differ from you could prove beneficial.

> If you are interested in learning more about the power of bringing together a diverse range of experiences and disciplines, please watch my six-minute TEDxNASA video at: www.ShapiroTEDx.com.

To help you build innovation teams where people of different styles and backgrounds come together in a high-performing way, I created Personality Poker. It is an incredibly fun and fast-paced card game that you can play with your team to make sure you are getting the best out of everyone. To learn more and get your decks, go to: **www.PersonalityPoker.com**

Test

The final step is "Test." The key to testing is not accepting failure as the norm but instead creating small, scalable experiments to test your hypotheses.

The concept of failure is now in vogue. It seems as though everyone is being told that in order to increase their level of innovation, they must fail more quickly and often. Although failure might be an inevitable outcome of innovation, it should not be the goal. We don't want to strive for failure. Instead, we want to become masters of experimentation so that we can minimize the risk. One of the primary causes of failure might surprise you.

We typically joke that "yeah, but" is the enemy of innovation. We've all been told that we need to stop uttering those words and replace them with "yes, and." But what if "yeah, but" is not the problem? What if there is something more insidious and less obvious? A bigger enemy of innovation is "wow, this is a great idea."

Falling in love with your own ideas is the surest way for them to fail. The main reason for this is confirmation bias. This is when the brain filters information and provides only the data that supports your beliefs, rejecting everything else.

We see confirmation bias in all areas of life. Our view of politicians and politics is driven by it. Your purchasing decisions are influenced by it. If you really want a particular car, for example, no number of bad reviews will change your mind. You will look at the positive ones and justify why the negative ones are wrong.

This happens in innovation too. When conducting experiments, if you believe your idea is great, you will only find evidence that supports that belief.

> But what if "yeah, but" is not the problem? What if there is something more insidious and less obvious? A bigger enemy of innovation is "wow, this is a great idea." Falling in love with your own ideas is the surest way for them to fail. The main reason for this is confirmation bias.

Scott Cook, the founder of Intuit, once said, "For every one of our failures, we had spreadsheets that looked awesome." This is brilliant! We can make any idea seem like a great idea. But the key to winning with innovation is to know which bets to place and which to avoid. Killing ideas is part of the innovation process. Knowing where to invest and where not to invest is critical. Of course, implementation doesn't end with experimentation. It is the first step. And it is a crucial step.

Making the Impossible Possible

With the FAST Innovation process, you now have the tools to start creating a high-performing innovation culture. Everyone in your organization will be on the same page about what is important, and they will be collaborating around differentiating opportunities that help

> Scott Cook, the founder of Intuit, once said, "For every one of our failures, we had spreadsheets that looked awesome."

you increase return on investment (ROI), drive higher levels of efficiency, and reduce overall risk. The next step is to take the concepts from this book and apply them to your organization.

Fortunately, innovation and problem-solving are not just for the so-called creative types. Anyone can participate. We are all innovative; we just innovate in different ways.

Walt Disney once said, "It's kind of fun to do the impossible." I, like many others, love a good challenge. But the effort does not need to seem Herculean.

Learn the tools provided in this book. Master the other steps of the FAST Innovation process. Use these approaches again and again, until they are inextricably linked with the DNA of your innovation process. I promise that you'll quickly move from the seemingly impossible to the possible and, ultimately, to the probable.

Why Innovation Is So Important to Me— and the World

Thank you for reading this far into the book. By now, I hope you understand the significance of the pivotal mindset for any organization, team, or individual. Along the way, I trust you've grasped not only what to do but also how to do it. However, I haven't yet shared the reason behind my deep passion for innovation—in other words, my "why." I hope that by understanding my motivation, you'll be inspired to further commit to innovation. We need it now more than ever.

In 1986, I graduated from Cornell University with a degree in industrial engineering and an emphasis in manufacturing productivity. My first full-time position was as a consultant for the global management consulting firm Accenture. Although I began my career focusing on technical computer tasks, I soon transitioned to work more aligned with my degree. In the early 1990s, I delved into process improvement

> The tipping point came in 1995 when I led a project for a major manufacturing company. Before we even began, the CEO announced that ten thousand people would be laid off due to our reengineering efforts.

initiatives to enhance company efficiency, a practice known as "business process reengineering."

We would assist companies with the optimization of their processes. We eliminated all inefficiencies. In theory, this should have had a positive impact.

However, I soon realized that when a company optimized its processes, it often resulted in a downsizing of the workforce. The tipping point came in 1995 when I led a project for a major manufacturing company. Before we even began, the CEO announced that ten thousand people would be laid off due to our reengineering efforts.

That was a staggering number, but I wasn't naive. I understood that people would lose jobs as we made companies more efficient. Somehow, I managed to rationalize the impact on the lives of so many. However, the devastating consequences of my work didn't truly hit me until one evening. After a long day, I returned to my hotel room and switched on the television.

The news program I tuned in to featured a story about three executives from my client's company who had lost their jobs a year earlier. These were leaders within the organization who had been handed pink slips.

The most optimistic of the three was an executive who had saved a significant amount throughout his career and recently received an inheritance. Even though he hadn't secured another job yet, he remained hopeful. Another executive was visibly emotional throughout the interview, being deep in debt and having resorted to mowing lawns to support his family. Tragically, the third individual had taken his own life.

The following day, while at the client's location, I confirmed that the stories were accurate. I immediately left the project and never looked back. After watching that television segment, I couldn't bear to contribute to even one lost job.

> Although the loss of ten thousand jobs didn't stir me enough to prompt change, witnessing the impact of a single job loss became unbearable.

Although the loss of ten thousand jobs didn't stir me enough to prompt change, witnessing the impact of a single job loss became unbearable.

I had an existential crisis.

It impacted me so deeply that I decided to take a six-month sabbatical to look back on my contributions to the world—both positive and negative. After several months of reflection, I had an epiphany: I wanted to shift gears. I no longer wanted to eliminate jobs; I wanted to create jobs. It was then that I decided to dedicate my business life to helping companies grow through innovation.

In 1995, innovation wasn't a popular topic in corporate hallways. But thirty years later, it's on everyone's lips. However, few truly know how to execute it effectively. That's why I am doubling down on my efforts to assist organizations—and individuals—in their innovation endeavors.

And I would love to help you master innovation. This is why I created my FAST Innovation® Mastery Program.

The FAST Innovation® Mastery Program

I remember a conversation with a woman who had been a client of mine for more than a decade. As she's always looking for the next big opportunity, she changed companies several times over the years. And each time when she went to a new organization, she would bring me in to do a speech, workshop, or training.

During a conversation, she said, "I'm tired of bringing you in any time we need help."

She said it with a bit of sarcasm and a lot of love. What she meant was that she wanted to build the capability internally, to replicate what I do and bring it into her organization.

We both knew that training was not the answer, as it was not deep enough or real-world focused. Speeches and workshops were not the answer, as they are episodic and don't build a long-term capability. And consulting was the opposite of what she needed since her goal was to clone me, not just get a one-time piece of advice.

Together, we created the first iteration of what is now my FAST Innovation Mastery Program. It is a deep dive into every step of the innovation process. But instead of two days in a conference room where people retain less than 10 percent of what they hear and apply almost none of it, we created an apprenticeship program that was spread out over an entire year.

For the first six months, I worked deeply with three people: the sponsor and two of her direct reports. Before we began, we identified some critical challenges and opportunities for the organization and also for the individuals. The goal was to not only solve these problems but to build the innovation muscle while doing it, applying the process to real-world problems that generate real ROI.

Every week for six months, I released content about my FAST Innovation process. This included videos, segments of books, and articles. The individuals (called Masters) consumed and applied what they learned. They used it with their opportunities. They shared it with their teams. And then, once a week, we hopped on a call where we talked about their successes, failures, and questions. No new content was delivered on the calls, only debrief and application.

This continued for six months.

Then, for the second six-month period, we got a larger group of twenty-four together. These were direct reports of the three individuals I worked with. Once a month, content was released to this larger group. The three Masters worked with the cohort (called Ambassadors) to help them apply the concepts. But rather than my leading the discussions, the Masters did this. And in the weeks between our monthly group calls, the Masters worked with the Ambassadors to help them apply the concepts and address any issues.

> The goal of the FAST Innovation Mastery Program is three-fold:
> 1. Generate real ROI by solving real-world problems and opportunities.
> 2. The ability to solve any problem now and forever.
> 3. Create a culture of innovation.

The goal of this program is three-fold:

1. Generate real ROI by solving real-world problems and opportunities. Solving just one problem will pay for the program many times over. Having the ability to do this over and over again is priceless.
2. The ability to solve any problem now and forever. You will build a capability that enables you to target, solve, and implement your most important opportunities without requiring outside support.
3. Create a culture of innovation. We don't stop with just a few individuals; we work toward scaling these capabilities throughout your organization. Not only does

this increase your ability to innovate, but it also creates an environment where employees are engaged and motivated so that they stay with you.

If you see the value of mastering depth in a world plagued by perpetual pivoting, then this program might be perfect for you. Discover more at:

www.FastInnovationMastery.com

On the page, you can schedule a consultation to delve into your innovation needs and challenges. Additionally, you can sign up to receive my article on how we created a twenty-thousand-person innovation practice at Accenture in just nine months. This approach, briefly outlined in the "Internal Dissemination" chapter, closely mirrors the one I use with my FAST Innovation Mastery Program.

I truly hope you will take me up on the offer for a consultation.

Continue the Journey

Thank you for reading to the end of this book. However, this doesn't have to be the end of our journey together. You can delve deeper into my work on innovation in many ways.

OTHER BOOKS AND PRODUCTS

Best Practices Are Stupid: 40 Ways to Out-Innovate the Competition (Amplify Publishing, 2023). Originally published in 2011 by Portfolio Penguin, this book includes forty different strategies for creating a culture of innovation. It covers a wide range of topics from strategy and measures to process and organization structures. The updated 2023 edition includes additional chapters, along with commentary on each of the forty tips. This book was selected as the best innovation and creativity book of the year when it was first published in 2011. The concepts are as relevant today as they were back then.

Invisible Solutions®: 25 Lenses that Reframe and Help Solve Difficult Business Problems (Amplify Publishing, 2020). When *Best Practices Are Stupid* was first published, many readers expressed curiosity about a tip titled "Don't Think Outside the Box; Find a Better Box." The point was that we should embrace the power of constraints rather than fight them. To do this, we need to master how to reframe problems and opportunities. *Invisible Solutions* provides the framework and tools for reframing any problem, paving the way for better solutions. Learn more at:

www.InvisibleSolutionsBook.com

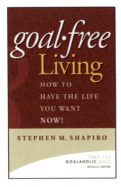

Goal-Free Living: How to Have the Life You Want NOW! (Wiley, 2005). Although it's not strictly a book on innovation, it was written to introduce innovation techniques into personal lives. I traveled across the United States and interviewed 150 creative individuals. During this three-month trip, I discovered that these innovators had a distinct approach to goals compared to others. I truly believe this book has the potential to be life-changing. Learn more at:

www.GoalFree.com

Personality Poker®: Contrary to conventional wisdom, opposites don't always attract. As a result, organizations hire and retain people who think alike. Although this uniformity is great for efficiency, it can stifle innovation. The key to high-performing innovation teams is ensuring that each individual is "playing to their strong suit" while the organization is "playing with a full deck."

Personality Poker is an interactive game that uses specially crafted cards. They look like regular playing cards, with one exception: each card also has a word representing a particular behavior, such as "creative," "analytical," "organized," or "empathetic." With fifty-two unique cards carrying fifty-two different descriptors, every element in Personality Poker—from the suits and colors to the numbers—has significance. Players trade cards to collect a hand of five that best reflects their self-perception. Additionally, players can "gift" cards to others. Based on the suits, colors, and numbers in your hand, you will discover:

1. Your preferred innovation personality
2. Your innovation unconscious biases
3. The people who you need to complement your hand yet most likely will avoid
4. What is missing from your team that is limiting innovation and success
5. The culture of your organization and its impact on innovation
6. How others perceive you and why any difference from your own perception can be damaging

… and much more.

Learn more at:

www.PersonalityPoker.com

SERVICES

Although books are a fast way to go deeper into my content, for greater impact, there are many ways that we can work together.

Keynote Speeches—For the past twenty-five years, I have delivered speeches in fifty countries. In 2015, I had the honor of being inducted into the Speaker Hall of Fame. My speeches extend beyond mere presentations. We conduct live hot seats, applying the concepts directly to your organization's real-world challenges in real time. Plus, all attendees receive materials that help keep the conversation going long after the event ends. Learn more at:

www.TheInnovationSpeaker.com

The FAST Innovation® Mastery Program—This is the most powerful and effective way to create a culture of innovation. Through our proven apprenticeship model, employees not only master the innovation process but also apply it to their daily work, addressing real-world problems. This approach both enhances employee competency and yields tangible ROI for your organization. Learn more at:

www.FastInnovationMastery.com

The FAST Innovation® Academy—If you are not quite ready for the FAST Innovation Mastery Program, our academy offers access to our entire content library without the cost of hands-on mentoring. This is ideal for organizations with tighter budgets or those aiming to quickly distribute the content to a broad segment of their organization. You can always upgrade to the mastery program in the future or add on levels of support. This program is under development. If you are interested in learning more, please get in touch with us at inquiries@stephenshapiro.com.

While browsing my website, please explore the various services I offer, including workshops, consulting, advisory services, and more.

About the Author

As I write these words about my past experiences, I realize two things: (1) This is of more interest to me than you, and (2) because of that, I don't expect you to continue reading. However, for the few interested in learning more about how I got to where I am, read on.

My career started after I earned a degree in industrial engineering from Cornell University. My focus was on improving manufacturing productivity. Although I didn't know it then, this was the perfect field of study for the work I would eventually do.

Right out of college, I joined Arthur Andersen's Management Consulting Division (now Accenture, the global management consulting firm). My first big career opportunity came in 1993 when I helped run our business process reengineering practice. This optimization work was a natural build on my industrial engineering work. Instead of improving manufacturing productivity, we focused on improving business productivity.

But as you discovered in the chapter about my "why," the resulting downsizing affected me emotionally. I chose to take a different path. Instead of helping companies shrink, I wanted to inspire them to grow. And since then, innovation has been my focus.

At that time, I was fortunate to be given the opportunity to found and lead a process and innovation practice of twenty thousand people. I gave speeches and workshops to consultants and clients around the world, promoting our perspectives on innovation. In 2001, I made a shift. I wrote my first book, *24/7 Innovation: A Blueprint for Surviving and Thriving in an Age of Change* (McGraw Hill). At that time, I left Accenture and branched out on my own. Since then, I've written six additional books—including the one you hold in your hands.

I have had the luxury of traveling the world, giving speeches in more than fifty countries. I am a Senior Fellow with The Conference Board, and in 2015, I was bestowed one of the highest honors of the speaking profession: I was inducted into the Speaker Hall of Fame.

When not speaking on stage, I enjoy practicing magic and making the impossible possible. Among my greatest celebrity coups, I met my childhood idol, former *Gong Show* host Chuck Barris. And in 2017, I got to be a judge and mentor on the TLC innovation reality television show *Girl Starter*.

I now live in Orlando, Florida, where I enjoy the most amazing life with my wife.

Acknowledgments

For me, writing the acknowledgments is always the most difficult part. Over the years, so many people have shared concepts, comments, and content that ultimately made their way into my books. Although it would be impossible to thank everyone who contributed, I want to recognize a few people.

The day I mentioned that I was writing another book, Adam Leffert was on the phone with me, providing valuable feedback on the cover, title, content, and nearly every aspect of the book. We exchanged hundreds of texts and emails over the past two years.

Andrea Kates, one of my innovation colleagues, was one of the first people to provide deep insights on enhancing the book's content at a macro level. Greg Satell contributed valuable feedback, insights, and statistics about innovation, including the Mercadona and Better Place stories. Brad Kolar has been an excellent sounding board for all my work over the past two decades, starting when we worked together at Accenture. Jon Fredrickson has supported me and my work for over fifteen years since we first met at InnoCentive. And Robert Richman was the genius who identified the connection between the word "pivot" and "pivotal," giving us the perfect one-word title.

In addition, countless beta readers and other advisors helped shape the content. Mary Brandon, Mark Hoffman, Arjun Yetukuri, Scott Winston, Bill Bullock, Paul Golding, Ping Zhong, Veronica McKee, Farhan Rafiq, Dan Kaus, Dave Cooper, Mariya Filipova, Curtis Michelson, Navin Kunde, Kaiser Yang, Matt Mueller, Briana Frank, Raj Gopalaswamy, Karen Tilstra, KC Shendelman, Dave MacAdam, Gareth Garvey, David Mucha, Amelia Schaffner, Helen Burns, Antonio Sanchez-Cordero, Paul Campbell, Maria Thompson, Joe Calloway, and so many others. I truly apologize if I left off your name.

Ela Aktay was the first editor of this book and coincidentally, she was the editor of my first book, *24/7 Innovation*. As always, she provided brilliant insights during the book's early formulation that shaped its structure and flow. I would like to thank AJ Harper and her author community, as well as her book, *Write a Must-Read*. They were instrumental in guiding me through the process. Additionally, a shout-out to Rob Fitzpatrick for his author community, his "Help This Book" software, and his book, *Write Useful Books*. His beta reader process was the one I used to get feedback early in the book's development.

The book you hold in your hands would never have been completed if it weren't for the amazing work of Naren Aryal and his team at Amplify Publishing. Lauren Magnussen, Will Wolfslau, Jenna Portnoff, Caitlin Schultheis, Josh Taggert, Nina Spahn, Sky Wilson, Josh Linkner, and others shepherded the book through the entire process.

Thank you to my parents for their support throughout my career and life.

And finally, as always, I want to thank my wife, Elénie, for her support and wisdom. She has made me a better person by opening my eyes and heart in so many positive ways. This has helped me grow as a husband, businessperson, and human being. Words could never express my deep appreciation for her, her guidance, and her love.